D0507173

How to Get Past Disappointment

Michelle McKinney Hammond

HARVEST HOUSE PUBLISHERS

EUGENE, OREGON

Unless otherwise marked, scripture quotations are taken from the New American Standard Bible®, © 1960, 1962, 1963, 1968, 1971, 1972, 1973, 1975, 1977, 1995 by The Lockman Foundation. Used by permission. (www.Lockman.org)

Scripture quotations marked NIV are taken from the Holy Bible, New International Version®, NIV®. Copyright © 1973, 1978, 1984 by Biblica, Inc.™ Used by permission of Zondervan. All rights reserved worldwide.

Verses marked ESV are from The Holy Bible, English Standard Version, copyright © 2001 by Crossway Bibles, a division of Good News Publishers. Used by permission. All rights reserved.

Verses marked NLT are taken from the Holy Bible, New Living Translation, copyright © 1996, 2004. Used by permission of Tyndale House Publishers, Inc., Wheaton, IL 60189 USA. All rights reserved.

Verses marked MSG are taken from The Message. Copyright © by Eugene H. Peterson 1993, 1994, 1995, 1996, 2000, 2001, 2002. Used by permission of NavPress Publishing Group.

Published in association with the literary agency of Alive Communications, Inc., 7680 Goddard Street, Ste 200, Colorado Springs, CO 80920. www.alivecommunications.com

Cover photo © Linden Lasema / stock.xchng

Cover design by Koechel Peterson & Associates, Inc., Minneapolis, Minnesota

HOW TO GET PAST DISAPPOINTMENT
Copyright © 2011 by Michelle McKinney Hammond
Published by Harvest House Publishers
Eugene, Oregon 97402
www.harvesthousepublishers.com

Library of Congress Cataloging-in-Publication Data
Hammond, Michelle McKinney.
How to get past disappointment / Michelle McKinney Hammond.
  p. cm.—(Matters of the heart series)
  ISBN 978-0-7369-3786-3 (pbk.)
  1. Christian women—Religious life. 2. Disappointment—Religious aspects—Christianity.
  3. Samaritan woman (Biblical figure) I. Title.
  BV4527.M4185 2011
  248.8'43—dc22
                                                        2010029891

All rights reserved. No part of this publication may be reproduced, stored in a retrieval system, or transmitted in any form or by any means—electronic, mechanical, digital, photocopy, recording, or any other—except for brief quotations in printed reviews, without the prior permission of the publisher.

Printed in the United States of America

11 12 13 14 15 16 17 18 19 / BP-NI / 10 9 8 7 6 5 4 3 2 1

To those who thought they could never love again,
smile again, hope again—think again.
There is hope for your life!
Follow your pain around the bend and look up...
truly all things come to pass.

Acknowledgments

To my dear Harvest House family. Thank you for always making me feel at home and giving me room to grow.

To all of those who have walked with me through the tears—you know who you are. I couldn't have made it without your prayers and care. I love you high, deep, and wide.

Contents

This is for all of those who have made the long walk to the wrong well and found it empty. Turn again and walk toward the sun. A stranger awaits…

> *Hope breaks forth from its prison*
> *like a butterfly stretching its wings to fly.*
> *It shakes off its coat of death*
> *experiencing new life*
> *Rising past disappointment*
> *and all that threatened to keep it bound*
> *It soars to meet its maker*
> *the author and finisher of its faith*
> *and heaven applauds*
> *the victory has been won…*

A Place Called Hope

W e all relate to thirst. The empty, yawning feeling you have inside that longs to be filled—filled with love, with accomplishment, with satisfaction and fulfillment. And yet so often it seems the very thing we pursue eludes us, teasing and taunting our hearts. Carrots are dangled just before our eyes to make us try, try again, only to be disappointed again and again until we refuse to try any longer or, worse, settle for the in-between.

Yes, somewhere between what we don't have and what we long for is a compromise that bides us over for a little while. But then what we truly want peeks around the corner of our longings to remind us that the dream hasn't been realized. We die a little with every reminder of this painful fact and search for ways to endure in spite of our disappointment in ourselves, in others, and even in God. We bolster our hearts and set our faces forward for the long haul and continue on…

We all come with our own special carry-on bag of survival tricks. Some people hide behind hectic schedules. Some engage in endless flirtations to distract from what they truly want. Like a wanna-be singer who hides behind the light show and the dancers onstage hoping we won't notice her tuneless delivery, we camouflage our true feelings. Scores of successful women flaunt their achievements while secretly mourning the lack of love or children in their lives. On the other side of the fence, many women flaunt their homes, husbands, and children while secretly coveting the achievements of women in the business world.

Disappointment is an ancient emotion. Truly there is nothing new under the sun. The Samaritan woman mentioned in John 4 could have been a woman living in our time. Perhaps she wouldn't have met Jesus at a well; it could have been a water cooler instead. The matters of the heart she struggled with are the same issues we deal with today. She can be the perfect study for us in how to refresh our faith and embrace new beginnings—while putting the past in the right perspective. Why not take the time to read her story before delving into this book? This will be a great overview to prepare for our journey together.

We all have pieces of fruit we feel we've been denied. And the serpent—the devil in disguise—makes sure we are frequently reminded of what we lack (or think we lack). Taunting us to agree with him that God is holding out on us. Pushing our attitudes over the edge until we land in a place that takes us further away from the place called Hope. And yet God promises there is hope for our lives. How we find it among the debris of disappointment remains a mystery to many. But rest assured, my dear sister. If God said it, it is so! Hope is only a prayer away!

PART 1

Who Am I?

When you look in the mirror who do you see? What does your reflection tell you about you? More importantly what do others read when they look at your face, your posture, the way you carry yourself? Our lives are written all over our faces. The choices we've made wear on us, drawing their wrinkles, creating furrows and laugh lines, telling their stories. The texture of our skin, the tension around our lips, the light (or lack of light) in our eyes reveals things we might never voice.

The glare of some of our choices and the consequences we've invited into our lives can be overwhelming at times, causing us to burrow deeper into a space that provides temporary comfort at best. But in this place is also something very dangerous—the absence of truth. Though the truth hurts it is also what brings the clarity we need in order to be free. We need truth. The absence of it creates bondage. Yet our hearts are deceitful. They shrink from the truth in favor of pride, yet God waits. He waits for us to come to the end of ourselves and our various disappointments and failings. He waits to extend His mercy when we throw up our hands and surrender, confessing what we know and what we do not know. In those moments the truth can lie buried under the layers of way too many experiences we've stuffed to a place called "I'll deal with it later" in the name of survival.

As God looks into our hearts the Holy Spirit does a deep and intimate search into the hidden places within and brings the things we harbor to light. Perhaps this is why we avoid encounters with God at times. Isaiah the prophet said it best. Sharing that he saw the Lord "sitting on a throne, lofty and exalted" the year King Uzziah died, Isaiah declared that he was a man of unclean lips and that he lived among unclean people (Isaiah 6:5). You see, when we truly draw close to God and see Him as He truly is, we also see ourselves as we truly are. All filters are removed. Not only do we see who we are, but we also come into the knowledge of what God requires of us. This which causes us to measure our ability to fulfill the call He places on our lives, and we are found wanting. All that we lack comes to the forefront, causing us to focus on the deficit within our souls. In the face of a holy God we are exposed, and all that we are and are not is revealed. Sometimes it's not a pretty picture. Who we perceive ourselves to be bears weight on how we respond to situations and people around us. Our self-perception often causes us to settle for standards below God's will for us based on what we believe we deserve.

Our conversations often reveal who we really are by revealing what we think. The Bible tells us that out of the abundance of the heart the mouth speaks. It unveils the things that lurk within us that we know or perhaps have not acknowledged. Yet they are there, manifesting themselves in every area of our lives. Our interactions with others. The way we love or hate. What we eat. Where we go. Who we associate with. The things we allow in our lives to go unchecked or uncorrected. The cycles that are repeated because we walk in denial of our part in the sequels that occur in our personal world.

The woman who keeps settling for terrible relationships, stays on a job she hates, or who never pursues her dreams is living out her self-perception. Deep within she has accepted what she thinks she deserves. Should something that would really make her happy come along, she would probably sabotage the opportunity. Though it is what she always wanted, deep within her psyche is a voice shouting, "You can't have that. You don't deserve it!" The truth is that none of us gets what we truly deserve in and of ourselves apart from Christ (thank our loving God for that!). This is what the redemptive power of God is all about. It redeems us to get what we don't deserve, but we must cash in the coupon God has given us to receive the gifts He so passionately wants us to have. He wants us to come clean with Him and with ourselves about who we truly are.

To get anywhere in this life on earth we have to be honest about ourselves. Though people around us may not be able to put their hand on what is missing, everyone knows what a lack of authenticity feels like. The people who lose the most are those who fail to be real. Not owning our stuff repels the grace God extends to us.

Yes, sometimes being honest with ourselves is difficult because life hurts too much. Repeat disappointments cause us to grow crusts over our hearts to shield ourselves from further pain. As this crust hardens and grows thicker, we can lose sight of our true selves, which leads to the inability to be in touch with our true needs.

What We Truly Value

"Who am I and what do I truly value?" Compromises begin if we can't honestly answer this question. We then justify our choices by comparing ourselves to others, and that's always dangerous. Comparisons magnify the things we believe we lack and batter our self-esteem. This is a contest we will never win.

The truth is there will always be someone smarter, more attractive, richer, whatever, than us. That's just the law of averages. But the most deceptive form of comparison is the one that magnifies what we believe we have so we can downplay what we know we don't possess. "Well at least I'm not like so and so," we say. We find fault in others to rationalize that we are all right, but our standards begin to slip inch-by-inch, increasing our unhappiness because deep within, our spirits know we aren't living God's best for our lives. Days stretch endlessly when we pace out our existence. Hope is diminished as we focus on what we don't have and discouragement sets in.

How do we turn the corner? It can happen in a moment—*the moment we choose to have an encounter with the One who knows us deeply and intimately.* The One who knows us better than we know ourselves. Only God can wash away our pain and renew our hope in Him and in ourselves. Strengthened and renewed, we are able to believe what seems impossible and receive the life God wants to give us—a life rich in righteousness, peace, and joy in the Holy Ghost. This is the ultimate in living in God's kingdom. To thrive whether we are in the desert, the valley, or atop a mountain because of who we are—Whose we are—and what we possess *in Him.*

Our knowledge of who we are in God insulates us from many of the assaults of life. We walk in the awareness of our kingdom rights and identities. We see ourselves and life through a different lens. This puts us in the position to embrace all that God has for us. To see it, to recognize it, to take hold of it. And not because we deserve it, but because it consists of gifts from our loving God, tokens of His love we receive freely.

Remember, who you think you are *might not be* who you really are. Your earthbound self merely hides your eternal personage. Your true identity is hidden in the One who created you. As you realize this and embrace who you are in light of who God is, authentic living begins and hope springs eternal.

Your Heart Condition

It was about the sixth hour.
When a Samaritan woman came to draw water.

❧

S he was hot—and not in a good way. Some thought she sauntered carelessly through the noonday sun, head held high, because she thought too highly of herself, had a chip on her shoulder, was just a bit too haughty for her own good. *She thinks she's something,* women muttered through clenched teeth and narrowed eyes as she walked past them.

In those moments she would lift her head even higher, thrusting forth her chin, wordlessly saying their opinions didn't matter. But deep inside they did—and more than she cared to admit. More than the arms of her lover could soothe her. More than the voices in her head that made excuses for the choices she'd made. Inside she died a million deaths. Her posture and attitude were her shields to fend off the telepathic arrows

15

that came her way from the people who hated her and what she represented. She was a prisoner in a life that couldn't be reversed.

And so she made adjustments to make life bearable. Weakness was not an option; she would not play the victim. Let them think what they would, she knew who she was. She would explain herself to no one. She had come to know that those who loved her didn't need explanations and those who didn't would never accept her anyway.

How ironic that in her ardent pursuit of love she found herself more isolated than ever. Growing weary of the silent conversations and condemnation that constantly swirled around her, she had relegated herself to solitude. Waiting until the sun rose to its highest point in the sky and punished all who ventured out beneath its gaze, she made her way to the town's main well to get the water she needed.

She was accustomed to the heat and relished having the area around the well to herself. The lack of tongues too busy, eyebrows raised in disapproval, and the careful-but-appraising gazes from some of the men was a relief. The well had become a place of solace. She welcomed the heat of the sun once she sat on the edge, splashing her face with water from the bucket she drew up. She arched her back and let the sun melt away the soreness in her muscles. Taking in the village before her, she reflected on the people who lived behind the shutters that had been put down to preserve the coolness within the homes. She wondered if they were happy. She marveled at how some of them had lived the same way, with the same person for years on end, while she always seemed to be forced into transition. Life seemed to have a will of its own, and it dragged her along unanticipated and painful twists and turns.

She often sat lost in thought, catching her breath before the trek back with the precious water. Sometimes she wondered how long she could continue this way. In those moments her shoulders would sag beneath the weight of the cares she tried to avoid most days. Then shaking it off like a garment too heavy to wear beneath the heat, she would stand and slowly head back to her dwelling. She fell back into disguise, deliberately swaying, creating her own rhythm, defying the harsh songs of the townspeople. Yes, she would sing her own song.

But this day was different. Her solitude was interrupted. A stranger sat on her prized spot. A flicker of annoyance crossed her face like the shadow of a leaf tossed in the wind. It was quickly replaced by a mask that revealed no expression. She harbored her irritation carefully. She had laid claim to the well and this time she chose because no one else would come. She hesitated, marking time, hoping the man would take her slow approach as a hint he should move on. She quickly glanced at him. He seemed planted to the spot, resting comfortably, and looking directly at her!

She could feel her back growing straighter under his gaze…a look she couldn't quite comprehend. It made her uncomfortable in a new way, which heightened her resentment of his presence. *Men: Can't live with them, can't live without them,* flitted through her subconscious. She had grown used to the stares of men so why was this man's gaze making her feel so defensive? She turned her back to him, seemingly looking for someone in the village. A frown creased her brow. She refused to let this stranger see her sweat or sense her feeling of being off balance. He was just a man. No big deal. She would ignore him until he moved on.

She sat down her jar and stretched, trying to occupy herself, willing him to move. Finally she picked up her vessel and turned. The man was still sitting there. *Well, just let him sit there. I have other things to do with my time besides get into a staring match. At any rate, I am not interested. He's kind of average looking. Humph. The nerve of this stranger to stare so brazenly.*

Like the woman at the well portrayed in John 4, there have been times in my life when I've been on the defensive before I knew if I had reason to be. Lost in my own questions, "Is this all there is to life? Is this to be my lot?" self-pity drifts aimlessly toward frustration. The shift of attitude can be so subtle. Anger gives way to apathy when we get tired of holding on to that much fire. It burns. And so we allow it to dissolve into cold embers. The anger that once made us feel strong is exhausting. To feel nothing is far less draining—or is it? Perhaps it depends on the time of day. At high noon when the heat is on in our lives, apathy is how we preserve the strength to draw another breath and move on. We learn to take the glare of life in stride, put on our sunglasses, and deal with it.

A friend once shared that her definition of disappointment is a "dissed" appointment. An appointment we made where the other parties intentionally or unintentionally didn't keep their end of the commitment. Add up the moments this has happened, and the layers begin to cover or perhaps even smother our spirits. We retreat beneath the layers, searching for comfort and escape from the pain of dreams unrealized and love unrequited. Imperceptible to us but apparent to others, accumulated disappointment becomes an unattractive veil that can be hard to take off.

I don't know about you, but I admit that at times disappointments have held my heart hostage, refusing to let me be free. My subconscious, involuntary reflex of self-protection blocked any possibilities of a repeat or even a new experience that might result in similar defeats. It was as if I'd drawn a heavy, suffocating, all-encompassing cloak over me, eliminating all signs of openness and inhibiting any interactions. I came across as a woman who was standoffish, had too much attitude, was unapproachable, and, even worse, might be arrogant and stuck on myself. I came across as the wrong kind of diva.

And none of that was true! In fact, it was the opposite of who I really am. The real problem was that I was too loving, too trusting, too generous, and too violated for my attempts at kindnesses. So I had collected my tattered toys to take them home where I alone could properly protect them. For this I was called selfish. There was no winning or losing. I learned not to care somewhere along the way—or so I thought.

Fortunately, God will not allow us to go on this way. There comes a day…a time…when He makes an appointment to meet us in our self-imposed quarantines to reconcile our past disappointments and inject us with hope once again so we will live life and embrace it fully. To feel what we feel and acknowledge it once and for all. To locate where we really are and move on.

Every life has reckoning points where opportunities present themselves as we continue on the path of life we've chosen. We decide whether we want to stay safe or dare to try one more time to be who we were created to be. A choice must be made once the challenge is issued. Hopefully in that moment of authenticity, the joy that eluded us will be realized.

Is there a reward for just being real no matter what? I think so…I hope so. It takes courage to strip away the layers of heart sickness that come from too many hopes deferred. Please keep in mind that pain is only the beginning of the journey and will soon dissipate. If we embrace it, we may be amazed at where it takes us!

And so we'll begin our journey together by stripping away the Band-aids and looking at our broken self-images through God's eyes as He stirs the water deep within the wells of our souls.

Reflections

1. What has been your greatest disappointment?

2. What cycles have you seen recurring in the area of disappointment?

3. In what ways have you responded to these cycles? To others around you? To new opportunities for love? To dreams?

4. What measures have you taken to protect your heart?

5. What other things might you subconsciously be protecting yourself from? How might this cost you?

6. How do you find the balance between wisdom and fear?

Refreshing Springs

When life is heavy and hard to take,
* go off by yourself. Enter the silence.*
Bow in prayer. Don't ask questions:
* Wait for hope to appear.*
Don't run from trouble. Take it full-face.
* The "worst" is never the worst.*
Why? Because the Master won't ever walk out
* and fail to return.*
If he works severely, he also works tenderly.
* His stockpiles of loyal love are immense.*
LAMENTATIONS 3:28-33 MSG

2

True Thirst

Jesus said to her, "Give me a drink."

His voice startled her. Though it was not loud. As a matter-of-fact, it was rather understated, mysteriously calming. It interrupted her thoughts, commanded her attention, and shattered her resistance. Still as she looked at this stranger she thought he had a lot of nerve. Didn't he see that she had just arrived at the well herself? What had he been doing the entire time he sat there? Why would he ask her for water when he knew she had none? Shouldn't he have offered to draw water for her? Perhaps he thought it beneath him—that drawing water was women's work. And also he was a Jew, she was a Samaritan, and everyone knew the two races didn't get along. She couldn't be certain at his rationale, but once again it uncovered wounds she had buried. Why did every man want something from her? It seemed that all of her life she had given and given until she found she had precious little left.

Not only was she hot, she was empty. Couldn't he see that? She stifled the urge to mirthlessly chortle. The man's "line" was such a pathetic attempt at conversation. Such an obvious excuse to begin an exchange. Obviously this stranger had no new tricks up his sleeve.

But she did. She stifled her automatic response to give what had been asked of her even when she didn't feel like giving. Not water. Not her attention. Not even a smile. Today would be different. She felt no compulsion to comply with his wishes.

She didn't know him, and he didn't know her. She was under no obligation to address his wishes. She didn't have to give him anything and she wouldn't—so there! She was taking charge of her own world. She was tired of people—men in particular—constantly placing demands on her. Inserting hollow reeds and sucking the life out of her. Blatantly calling attention to their needs while completely ignoring hers. Making her feel guilty about taking care of herself first. It was an effective strategy. She would chide herself for being selfish and once again pour out of her limited reserves the care they asked for. The time they insisted on. The empathy she could no longer feel. She was done. So done that she was tough. Inflexible. Hard on the outside like an overcooked dish left too long under the glare of flames too hot.

She had developed a crust that could not be penetrated. Oh, she knew how to act as if she cared at the right times. She could pantomime her well-rehearsed "life is just fine as it is" role to get by. It was called survival. Moving on automatic. Going through the motions without the emotions. "A woman's got to do what a woman's got to do" was her mantra. She felt as if she were suffocating behind the walls she had fashioned with her own hands. She wanted out of her self-constructed prison, but she could no longer see even a pinprick of light to guide the way.

Coming back to the present she wondered why this near-silent stranger irritated her so deeply. He had only asked one question. He wasn't being pushy, insistent, or belligerent. She couldn't quite put a finger on why his quiet request pushed so many internal buttons. Why did such a simple request make her so upset? She did have a choice after all. She could give him what he asked for or say no. She pondered why she felt so unsettled. His request felt like a loaded question, but she didn't understand why. She sensed that water from the well wasn't what he was truly after. She felt naked. Ashamed. Lacking. Why was she embarrassed before this stranger?

She would never let him know how he affected her, how he had penetrated her façade of self-sufficiency, how he had ruffled her carefully cultivated cocoon that insulated her from pain. She tilted her chin upward, deflecting his question by turning the focus from herself back to him. Let him be the one to squirm. He was the one who was out of place.

Don't you just hate it when someone asks you for something you don't have? Especially when that someone is God. Your friends may not know the depth or absence of your reserves, but surely God does. Is He being cruel when He highlights our lack by asking for the very thing He knows we don't have? Why does He do that? Why does God ask such hard questions when He already knows the answer?

I suppose it is far kinder to ask than to blatantly expose. When we see God's questions in this light, it's rather endearing. He is giving us the option to empower ourselves and come clean about where we are, who we are, and what we are—empty vessels that need to be filled by Him.

His questions not only expose us, they also test us. Are we willing to stretch beyond where we are presently? They highlight our need until it is glaringly evident, creating a hunger in us for more than what we've experienced thus far. This is the gentle leverage God uses so we'll squirm in our discontent and seek Him. He wants more for us than what we've settled for.

Ah, but that is the rub, is it not? Faith is required to receive what we want from God. We have to trust before we'll reach out and expose our needy hearts. God knows more about what is hidden in the recesses of our souls than we do. Just when we think we are fresh out of love, He stretches us to extend ourselves one more time in sacrificial love for someone. And His love flows through us. Just when we think we have no more time, strength, or even resources, He urges us to dig even deeper and reach out to someone in need. That is where He strengthens us—in the middle of the stretching and digging.

In the book of 1 Kings is an amazing story that shows what God can and will do for us. A destitute widow was approached by God's prophet Elijah. He asked her for a drink and a little bit of food because God had told him she would provide for him. The widow had just enough for her son and her, but Elijah encouraged her to fix his meal first... and then use what was left for her and her son. She did as he asked, and then he revealed God's promise to her because of her sacrificial obedience: "The jar of flour will not be used up and the jug of oil will not run dry until the day the LORD gives rain on the land" (1 Kings 17:14 NIV). God asks us to pour out the last of our oil and flour so we can discover and experience His ability to supply our needs. He is truly the God of more than enough!

Reflections

1. What are you fresh out of spiritually?

2. What do you feel you are asked to give time and time again?

3. *In what ways have the demands of others wearied you?*

4. *What areas do you need God to refill or refresh in your life?*

5. *Is there anything you can do to keep from being depleted?*

Refreshing Springs

When you feel you have nothing left, call on God and look again. Love again. Give again. When the initial step is taken, you'll find you have more than you realize because God shows up in that moment to breathe life on your offerings and increase them in measures beyond your imaginings. This reminds me of the words to an old song "He Giveth More Grace" by Annie Flint: "For out of His infinite riches in Jesus [God] giveth, and giveth, and giveth again." Truly His mercies are new every morning (Lamentations 3:22-23)! As His grace kisses your needs, you'll find you have more than enough.

3

In Search of Identity

*"How is it that You, being a Jew, ask me for a drink
since I am a Samaritan woman?"*

❦

Who is this person? the woman at the well thought. Either he was crazy or simply had no knowledge of protocol. Even she knew that he wasn't supposed to be speaking to her. He, after all, was a rabbi. She could tell by his clothing. He was definitely a Jew, and Jews usually wanted nothing to do with Samaritans. Most went out of their way to skirt this town on their travels even if it meant going miles out of their way.

This Samaritan woman had been taught early in life to accept her station. She had several strikes against her. She was a woman. A single woman. A single woman living with a man. She was a Samaritan. She was the wrong gender, race, and religion for that time. She was living the wrong lifestyle. She was the wrong everything.

Her personal history confirmed what the voices inside of her were saying. And when she didn't listen to them, she had the peanut gallery of her neighbors and the town's "good" citizenry to remind her that she was worthless. She tilted her chin upward again. There were days when this indictment affected her more than others. Some days she rebelled by pushing back, deflecting their hurtful arrows by casting aspersions on those who were "haters." Sure it was tit-for-tat, but sometimes it was entertaining and took the sting out of their comments and stares...and egos.

Still the truth of the matter was glaringly evident. She was a second-class citizen with very little value...and seen as someone who offered nothing to society. Besides a meal and a warm body for her lover, that is. She longed to make a difference. To do or say something of worth that would change people's lives. That was her private dream.

And here was this stranger speaking to her as if she were his equal. How could that be? Jews despised and looked down on Samaritans. They believed Samaritans were the armpits of society—unenlightened and not worthy of attention from their God. What did this Jew want? What was he up to? His motives had to be questionable, of this she was certain.

She was confused by his demeanor. He didn't seem like he was out to trick her or harm her. But just in case, she would remind him of protocols.

His face didn't change as she went down her list of disqualifiers. That bewildered her even more. Didn't he get what she was saying? She was uneasy. She wasn't used to being treated with respect. She felt afraid. She suddenly realized she'd drawn strength and comfort in being an outcast. It freed her from the responsibility of making a difference and having to continually make the choice to conform or not to conform. No excuses were needed for not doing anything. No rationalizations were needed if she stayed in the shadows. These disturbing thoughts could disrupt her life forever. Was she ready for that? She wasn't certain.

So much of our lives are spent as prisoners of self-perception. Our self-view comes from comments about us we've heard and what we've experienced because of who we are as we grew up. There is a marked contrast between a child who is encouraged to dream big and achieve versus the child who is told he or she can't succeed or achieve anything worthwhile and is berated with comments like "Who do you think you are?" The underlying message being the child thinks too highly of himself. There is also a strange type of "pride in humility" that many are taught. The misguided notion that others should notice their humility and follow suit makes me chuckle. After all, a person who is truly humble never feels humble enough.

To be confident in ourselves as people created by God with special gifts and talents coupled with faith and prayer for guidance paves the way for us to realize our hopes and dreams without being arrogant. I believed I was quite the ugly duckling growing up. I can still recall my shock when someone first told me I was beautiful. I didn't believe it. I got angry, believing he was making fun of me. *Doesn't he know it isn't nice to tell someone she's beautiful when she's not?* I thought. Although I had matured and blossomed, the old recording that said I was ugly still played in my head. I hadn't embraced a new perception. I still carried myself in a way that apologized for my unsightliness.

In later years I finally accepted that I was attractive, but I still compensated for that confidence by focusing on my battle with weight. And even when I lost weight, I hid under layers of clothes, giving the appearance that I was bigger than I was. When I finally came out from under the shroud I was amazed by the positive comments about my figure. This is just one of countless examples of how we disqualify ourselves from being blessed, getting ahead in life, and even getting the love we so deeply desire and need.

Jesus was very secure in who He was. His security was not in Himself but in who had sent Him. He knew who He was because of who He was connected to, part of, related to and why He was here. When people accused Him wrongly and betrayed Him, He wasn't distracted. He didn't break character because He was certain about His identity.

He understood that His mission would not change or be averted simply because someone didn't agree with Him. He knew that His power and His value wouldn't diminish if no one received Him or believed Him.

In moments when I suffer from insecurity, I pause and think about this. It's easy to miss out on the love I'm looking for if I don't feel lovable. To miss out on that business opportunity if I don't believe in myself or my ideas. Self-perception is a major part of winning any prize or battle. What we think of ourselves drives our attitude. Our attitude drives our actions. Our actions invite reactions, which may or may not reinforce our thoughts, which ultimately sets us on the course that affects our habits, our lives, and our character.

It is so liberating to get to the point when no one's opinion matters but God's. Then we're driven by a greater sense of purpose than what anyone has ever told us. Jesus said, "Do not fear those who kill the body but are unable to kill the soul; but rather fear Him who is able to destroy both soul and body in hell" (Matthew 10:28). We need to stay focused. The negative voices around us and in our heads are distractions from the real point of why we are here. When we listen and follow the negative voices instead of moving forward on the course God sets for us, we have only ourselves to blame. We get to take full responsibility for choosing to go outside God's guidance. We are often our own worst enemy! Every day we choose to be a victim or a victor based on which voice we choose to listen to. Please choose wisely.

Reflections

1. If you had to write a short intro for yourself, what would you say?

2. What have others said about you? What is true? What is untrue?

3. How have the opinions of others colored your perception of yourself?

4. How do your thoughts line up with what God says about you? How do they differ?

5. What scriptures can you read and memorize to renew your mind and transform your attitude?

Refreshing Springs

You can rejoice that in Christ you come into the fullness of who you were designed to be. The things that were impossible in your own strength are totally possible when you partner with God. His peace will sustain you. His grace will equip you. His joy will strengthen you. When you become part of His immediate family, you are validated, affirmed, and counted worthy of the significance you desire. In Him your identity and value are secured. You are the daughter of the King of kings!

PART 2

Who Is He?

Who is Jesus? Our perception of who God is and His intentions toward us color our attitudes, affect our judgments and choices, and lay the foundation for everything that occurs in our lives. Our perception of who God is and what part He plays in our lives will either wreak havoc on our destinies or bless us beyond our wildest dreams.

We humans are conditioned to make judgments in light of what we know and experience. For those who have had an absentee father, the concept of a heavenly Father being someone who is always present and always loving can be hard to grasp. If you've lived with a string of broken promises, it's hard to trust in the faithfulness of God. Whatever has been modeled for us in our significant relationships is what we tend to believe about God. And yet He transcends all earthly relationships. He is not bound by mortality or humanity. He is not flawed; He is perfect. He is the only One capable of having perfect relationships with us.

But there is one problem. We are imperfect people in search of perfect relationships. We hold others to standards we can't live up to. Only one person can—God. Based on how open we are to God's concept of love, our faith in who He is, and what He means for us personally, we can experience love perfected from Him.

So let's take a look at God and unpack who He is. This issue is huge. Many religions paint a very different picture of God, relegating Him to being impersonal and spiteful. But when we embrace a personal relationship with God through Christ, we have an up-close view of God's heart. This is what enables us to believe in and depend on Him, giving us victory in our day-to-day lives.

Proverbs 9:10 states that "the fear of the LORD is the beginning of wisdom." "Fear" doesn't mean "terror," in this verse. It is more of a "healthy awe and reverence" for a holy God and all His attributes. It indicates an understanding of His power and who we are in light of His Lordship. It is a willing surrender to His way because we understand that it is best for all involved. All these things bring wisdom to our world. We make our choices based on our understanding of these foundational issues. When we embrace this understanding, we move past fear to faith, to love, to glad obedience. Indeed, Jesus said, "If you love Me, you will keep My commandments" (John 14:15). Did you get that? He didn't say, "If you go to church…read your Bible…have born-again parents…believe God exists." No, Jesus said simply a heart motivated by love for Him will willingly acquiesce to the instructions of the Spirit of the Lord. No, it is not enough to be in awe of God or even to worship Him. Fear *will not* sustain obedience. Love and hope are the passions that fuel our willingness to resist the pull of the flesh and respond to the call of God's Spirit urging us toward holiness and sound living.

I've also pondered the "fear of the Lord" in another way that's been helpful. "Fear of life without the Lord" is also the beginning of wisdom. The vast hopelessness this thought implies is overwhelming. Although there was a point in my life when I had no intimacy with Christ and didn't seek His counsel, I shudder at the thought of life without Him today. My life was a mess; my choices senseless and erratic at best. The difference between my life then and now is markedly different. The absence of true light versus the presence of it accompanied by perfect love and divine intelligence has made all the difference in my world.

And yet we must trust before we will willingly obey. To follow a command given, we always consider the source. For instance, we will never choose to obey someone who means us ill unless we're forced to. So to trust God, we need to know who He is—and not just by hearsay or on the words or teachings of others. We need to go beyond religious tenets to get up close and personal with Him. And once we've had a personal encounter with Jesus and accepted Him as our Savior and Lord, no one can take that away from us or rearrange our view of Him without our consent.

Once we've entered into a personal relationship with Jesus, there must be continuous interaction to create a track record between God and us that solidifies our trust and willing response when He gives us instruction. Think about it. We gladly take the advice of someone that we know loves us and has the best of intentions toward us. Sometimes we wrestle with the fact that God knows the plans He has for us but doesn't tell us. We don't know what He is doing, and because of our need to control our circumstances and our fear of the unknown, we can lapse into being distrustful of the very One who has the best of intentions toward us. So we want to make sure we know God intimately and stay in touch regularly.

God urges us to draw close to Him. If there are issues that separate us, He invites us to come and reason with Him, confess our sin, and allow Him to wash us and make us righteous in Him. As we draw close and are restored by His redemptive power, He reveals His heart. He is restoration. Generosity. Healing. Deliverance. He is close to the brokenhearted and those bowed over in spirit. He longs to be near and apply His healing balm to soothe our pain and calm our fears. He wants us to know we have hope in Him.

If our only lens for seeing Him is through the experiences we've had with people, especially men, family, or close associates, we might miss the power and beauty of what a true, loving relationship with Christ is all about. Intimacy on this level is almost incomprehensible to us. We can have solid trust in Him and never be disappointed because God is Spirit, not human—He doesn't lie, doesn't flicker or change, doesn't hedge on His promises. He does what He says and says what He means. He is ever faithful even when we are faithless. He is tender and merciful. He sees the best part of us—through Christ—and He never gives up on us even when we let Him down. His love is unending and unconditional. The meter of how He loves us never decreases. In spite of us, He loves us.

Many men and women have spent exhaustible times pouring themselves—all their hopes, dreams, and emotions—into people, creatures, objects, and philosophies that don't give the return they were hoping for. These temporary wells of fulfillment evaporate with time or difficult circumstances. Emptiness and thirst for something more returns, driving them to pursue other sources to fill the void that only God can fill. Again and again this cycle repeats itself, and they find themselves more bereft with each fresh disappointment. Only One person can break this relentless cycle and bring new beginnings and true refreshment.

We must see God as He is and approach Him in light of that beautiful truth. The truth of His love and passion for us. The good intentions He has toward us. His faithfulness to His promises and His determination that we be victorious and joined to Him. This realization gives us new identities in Him, along with new purpose and new hope.

With God we have something to look forward to beyond this life, and yet He gives us powerful reasons to be living today. When we know Him and trust Him to be the source of all we seek, our dependency on things that disappoint wanes, and we are sustained by the higher and greater promises that come from the One who always keeps His Word. This is the living water He promised. He rewards us with His presence and blessings as we seek Him. Our spirits are quenched as we discover Him as more than Lord, more than King, more than Savior—as the Lover of our souls. We rest in His arms because we are His and He is ours.

4

It's Not About You

*Jesus answered and said to her, "If you knew the gift of God,
and who it is who says to you,
'Give Me a drink,' you would have asked Him,
and He would have given you living water."*

❧

*D**idn't the stranger understand?* she thought. *I'm not qualified to receive any gifts from God.* And yet her curiosity was piqued. *What
gift? Who is this stranger who seems so confident in who he is that it magnifies everything I know I'm not?*

The thought of receiving a gift from God was overwhelming. She
wondered if God was that generous. In her mind He was high and
lofty, requiring perfection from afar. She had long ago decided she
wouldn't ever measure up. Yet something inside longed to know that
she could touch Him and that He could touch her…would *want* to
touch her heart.

She often wondered if God heard her prayers. Or if her lifestyle and past disqualified her from consideration. She hoped He heard. This was a thread of mercy she clung to. And now this stranger sat there calmly telling her that it wasn't about her at all. Instead, it was all about who God was.

This set her back. She had to stop and ponder. What did she really think about God? Was He completely good? She'd never given it much thought. She knew what she'd been taught about God, but she had no intimate experience she could use as a reference. She did as she was taught, that was all. She went through the motions without emotion like most everyone lest she incur God's terrible wrath. But God being generous? God giving gifts to her personally? The almighty God listening to her and caring about her? These were foreign thoughts.

"Living water?" I've never heard of it. It sounds good and refreshing, she decided. Her insides ached suddenly, as if crying out for what this stranger spoke of. *What would I have to do to get that living water? Nothing is free...especially from men.* His statement seemed to suggest that she only had to ask. That this gift wasn't based on qualifications or actions. No, the gift was only about God and His generosity. She struggled to grasp this concept. A generous God who had something she wanted. Not only did He have it, He wanted to *give* it to her just because. How could that be true? That made Him sound real...a solid presence who wanted to interact with her. Had she heard about this part of God before? She didn't think so.

Unconsciously she moved closer to the man by the well. She looked up at him...into his eyes. She saw nothing but kindness and compassion...and something else...something that said "You can trust me."

The sun seemed hotter than ever, magnifying her thirst as she lingered on the idea of "living water." She imagined plunging into a pool of fresh, clear water, being completely immersed momentarily. *Would "living water" wash away all the pain I've experienced?* she wondered. *Could it replace all the tears I've cried? "Living water" seems like a lofty promise, but if he was bold enough to promise such a thing, he must have access to it. Why would he make such a claim if he didn't?* Still, other men had promised her things before and not delivered.

꿏

There have been times I couldn't see God because I was too distracted by me. Looking back I realize it was too much of me and not enough of Him. In those moments when I am overwhelmed with myself, I plummet to the depths of a dry well where my lack is magnified. I despair and go deeper inside myself—and find nothing. When I determine I have nothing to give, I feel disqualified to receive. Herein begins the race toward independence as I try to fulfill myself so I can receive. This propels me down a path that leads nowhere near what I was looking for. I crumple in a heap at the end of my effort.

I feel my shame disqualifies me from even reaching out to God. He couldn't possibly love me now that I've rejected Him in lieu of chasing my own desires and fulfillment. Satan, the accuser, taunts and torments, declaring me of no further good or interest to God. My desperation heightens, and I try to make the most of being on my own. After all, what doesn't kill a person makes that person stronger, right? And in those moments God reaches out. He blesses me in spite of myself. I am humbled. He wants me to know that even when I am not true to who He created me to be, He will remain true to who He promised to be in my life. Whew! I'm relieved even as I realize this is too deep for me to grasp.

How profound that the God of the universe, the One who created all things, would pursue me in my unworthy state and choose to bless me with good things. I fluctuate between being relieved that I've not received what I really deserve because of my sins and being humbly embarrassed at His overwhelming generosity in spite of my unrighteousness. And this is where I learn the most profound lesson about me: I am petty and small. I'm quick to be offended and withhold blessings when others don't cooperate with my wishes. Oh how I long to be more like God—gracious in the face of rejection and consistent in my love even when those I love are being unlovable. It's so hard not to judge, not to think about what others deserve for their lack of consideration. I've decided who wasn't worthy of receiving my time, love, and attention in the past, but now the goodness of God breaks my heart. My heart suffers when I see the wounds of those around me now. I finally realize they aren't giving me what I want because they can't. They can't be my source of happiness, achievement, or success.

Did you notice that the woman at the well had no water to give when Jesus asked for a drink? She would have to draw the water from the well first. And time and time again, I've discovered that when I feel I have nothing to give I find myself staring into the eyes of my gracious God, who extends to me what I can't offer others because I am broken and dry. I weep at the thought, first out of shame and then out of gratefulness that God's heart is large enough to love me, flaws and all. His compassion and care continue to surprise me. In spite of the times that He isn't my first "go to" resource, He still longs to give me good gifts. Gifts I don't deserve. Only One being is so secure in who He is that He can always love even when rejected, give even when love is withheld, and forgive the unforgivable. Only one—only God. I reach out my hands for what He gives, knowing I will never comprehend the immense love and grace He gives to me. I drink in His mercy and simply say, "Thank You, Father. I love You."

Reflections

1. How accepting are you of God's grace?

2. Does anything hinder you from receiving from Him? Explain.

3. Who do you look to first when you thirst for love and completion?

4. Who is God to you? What part does He play in your fulfillment? Is there a missing link in your relationship with Him?

5. How will you increase your knowledge of God this week?

Refreshing Streams

Perhaps you struggle with knowing who God is because you're afraid to be open with Him. And yet He already knows you completely. The overwhelming and scary fact that God knows everything about you, including your thoughts and motivations, yet still loves you and pursues you for a more intimate relationship is hard to fathom, but it's true! This reality is so rich with possibilities. Jesus wants you to experience complete love and fulfillment in Him. He only needs one thing from you: an invitation to enter your heart and life as your Lord and Savior. Have you asked Him in yet?

5

Encounters

She said to Him, "Sir, You have nothing to draw water with."

She sniffed as she noted aloud that he couldn't have living water because he had nothing to contain it. *He has a lot of nerve making such a lofty promise. And didn't he just ask me for a drink! What kind of game is he playing?* She masked her confusion with a calm façade. *What gives him the right to think he knows my needs or is qualified to meet them? How dare he!* Her mind skipped across her past relationships the way a pebble bounces across the surface of a lake, ripples disturbing the smooth-as-glass water and sending flashes of light by reflecting the sun. Names and faces emerged in kaleidoscope fashion stirring a turmoil of emotions with each haunting memory. So many people had promised her things and never delivered. Love, security, happiness, peace...all were so fleeting. And now this rabbi, who shouldn't even be speaking to her in public, was extending an impossible offer with no evidence that it could be fulfilled. But still...

The man had asked her for water, but then he said he had water. And to top that off, he was indicating that his water was better than what she could get—it was *living* water, whatever that means. What is it with men? Why couldn't they just be and allow relationships to unfold if they will, little-by-little. They seem to always make promises they can't keep to hurry things along.

She'd finally positioned herself so she didn't look back at the disappointing past or forward to the nebulous future. She would no longer be disappointed by the present choices in front of her. If she controlled her circumstances, she could avoid giving way to hopes that would never be fulfilled. She no longer waited for others to let her down; she assumed they would and hardened her heart. She cut off anyone who wanted to make empty promises.

So she let this strange Jewish man know she knew he really wasn't offering anything. He had nothing to hold this "living water" in! She wasn't going to fall for false hopes and promises. He wasn't equipped to offer her anything. This time she would do them both a favor and not get involved. She would not accept his invitation to drink water because it was obvious he couldn't provide any. And she refused to get into a debate about how he would deliver the impossible.

She smiled slightly. This was a small victory for her. So many times she'd believed what people said, trusting them—expecting them— to deliver on their promises. And their failure shattered her heart, her hope, her ability to love. She was left with an ache that filled her heart and soul. This time would be different.

There is a place called "beyond caring," located just past "repeated disappointments." It's dark and lonely there. And the hope and courage to expect something new and positive are lost on the road getting there, bankrupting our capacity for faith and leaving us stranded in our emptiness. This is when we decide we have to take control, to make life happen. But in our desperation the choices we make sabotage our intended outcomes as we battle the original desires that were never met and play tug of war with the feelings of despair that threaten to drown us.

I've been there, my friend, just like you have. We feel forsaken by God and mankind. We don't dare to trust either. We take our lives and hearts into our own hands, looking for protection and relief. The voices of doubt surround us, growing louder and louder. We're paralyzed in the midst of clinging to our own devices and choices we hope will provide escape. They fail and we surrender the last shred of faith. We struggle to regain our footing, realizing that there is another way... something beyond ourselves. Do we dare hope? Do we dare reach out and ask God for help? To trust Him for fulfillment? It's hard to humble ourselves. To believe that our sense of "omnipotence" is really *impotence,* especially in the face of His greatness.

We've reached a fundamental truth. Who we are comes down to who God is in our lives. It is only when we dethrone ourselves that the possibilities for fulfillment open and become obtainable. When we give up our futile attempts to seek love and joy from sources that have no power to give us what we're looking for, we finally turn to God.

I've been guilty of that. I have sought fulfillment in relationships with men. I have sought validation from accomplishments. I have sought joy from purchases I could not afford. I've looked for affirmation from friends and readers of my books, and sought peace from my own assurances. The problem with all of these resources is they are limited and will fail many times. Love relationships have left me wanting and hurting, reeling from the betrayals and disappointment of discovering someone wasn't truly who they said they were, pretended to be, or who I thought they were.

I have a friend who is an avid networker. She flits from event to event, person to person, hoping her connections will give her what she needs to further her vision. Promises abound and much too much energy and time are spent on those who use her without delivering any of the things she needs to complete her own work. Her disappointment is palpable as she questions God, questions the integrity of people in general, and questions herself. I remind her that she continually sets herself up for disappointment.

As I go down the list of the areas where strides have been made in her work, a common thread becomes evident. The things she has received didn't come from the sources she spent so much time and effort trying to glean from. They came from unexpected places. This is so like God! I pointed out this profound evidence of His ability to provide in His own way and time. What a commentary on His faithfulness and consistency.

We both paused and reflected on this. Truly God was active in what she was doing and was more than interested in supplying her needs. He is generous. He wants to give us good and perfect gifts that are fulfilling and sustainable. That's the bottom line. And when that information moves from our heads to our hearts and becomes part of us, our entire posture changes. We find ourselves miraculously refreshed again and again by all that comes and flows from reveling in His presence. And, finally, we learn who to turn to when we thirst.

God has promised us that He is the rewarder of those who diligently seek Him, and that He is our great and exceeding reward. He chooses to be available for our refreshing, healing, and wholeness! Unfortunately, we are so often distracted by our yearnings we fail to see Him and the unlimited possibilities He offers. Let's quit groping in the dark for His light. Like the man who cried to Jesus, "Help my unbelief!" we can ask God to refill us when our faith feels depleted. He is ever faithful and will meet us in our need every time, reminding us that He is the best thirst-quencher of all. The longer we stay at the well drinking His living water, the longer our souls will be satisfied. Let's turn our eyes toward the One who always satisfies.

Reflections

1. *What promises have been made and broken in your life?*

2. *What is your usual response when your expectations aren't fulfilled?*

3. *What conclusions do you draw?*

4. *How does disappointment affect your expectations of others?*

5. *How can you be free from being disillusioned?*

Refreshing Springs

Every time I've been disappointed, I've eventually noticed I was looking in the wrong place and seeking the wrong source. Yes, there have been times when I didn't want God to be my reward. I wanted what I wanted. But what I want apart from Him never satisfies for long. If the reward doesn't come from His hand, the joy is worthless and unsustainable. It becomes dry and lifeless. And worst of all, it is unfulfilling. Have you experienced this?

Jesus is the only One equipped and qualified to fulfill your deepest yearnings. He knows what you want and what you truly need. He will do an amazing and beautiful work by providing both. When you wait on Him, turn your focus to Him and all that comes from His hand, then you'll find what you're looking for. And many times it won't be what you thought it would be!

He satisfies the thirsty and
fills the hungry with good things.
PSALM 107:9 NLT

6

A Refreshing River

*The well is deep; where then do You
get that living water?*

Even as she told the man that the well was deep and asked about the
living water, she wondered which well she was talking about—
the well next to them or the empty chasm inside her heart that bore
through to the bottom of her soul. As she breathed in the hot, arid air,
she felt it whistle through her being, leaving a fine coating of desert
dust settling on her spirit and all the disappointments she had buried
within her heart. There were so many things she'd never cried about.
There had never been time as she hurried past her hurts to attain what
she needed to survive.

She wondered if the weariness she felt showed. Sometimes she
would stand in front of the mirror trying to read the eyes of the woman

who stared back at her. She searched the lines of the stranger's face... her face...for the telltale signs of dark secrets that had never been revealed. Had her exterior registered anything that might give away what she fought so hard to keep hidden?

She couldn't really discern anymore what caused the most discomfort—the pain of failures and disappointments or her shame. The lines of demarcation were paper thin, especially with her tears blurring the lines. Yes, her internal well was very deep. After years of stuffing disappointment, betrayal, rejection, and devastating losses, she felt a yawning expanse of nothingness.

Her one consolation had been the certainty that she would do whatever she had to. She would survive. Was she selling herself short? Probably. But she'd become accustomed to closing the eyes of her heart and fixing her gaze on something pleasant to distract herself from the present reality. Whatever adjustments had to be made to ensure her security, well, they just had to be made. This was her lot in life, and she had accepted it...and even achieved moments of numbness she called peace.

Until this stranger had come along. He was suggesting there was something more, something about living...about life. And he seemed to be offering it to her! She wondered if he was speaking double talk. Was living water really water or something else?

She looked up at him and saw a glimmer of comprehension in his eyes at her assessment of the deepness of the well. Did he know she was thinking about the deep well inside her heart and soul? Yes, he must. She sensed empathy in his gaze...or was it wishful thinking on her part? Could anyone comprehend the depths of her pain and longing? And if he did, what could he do about it? Did she dare to hope that he could stop the gnawing inside her? Could he fill the void? Repair the breaches in her faith? Where would he get this magical water? Does he really have access to such water?

Too many questions were swirling through her head. She fought against the hope that was trying to surface in her heart. *Hope brings pain*, she told herself. *But yet...* No! She wouldn't—couldn't—go there.

She would not set herself up for disappointment again. It cost too much to hope her life could change for the better. She spoke to herself as if addressing a petulant child who didn't understand the cost of what he wanted. *You've been coming to this well for years and years, and the water always tastes the same. It's regular water. Why should today be any different?*

I've been there. Have you? I've packed up my heart and refused to play anymore because the cost was just too much. The pain was too agonizing. I have cut many people and activities off at the pass out of fear that they might resemble painful situations from the past. I was no longer willing to let scenes play out to see if the storyline would take different turns. I'd been to that country before and taken enough photos to last me a lifetime. I had no interest in going back. The phantom pain I still carried was a very real reminder of why I should stay safe. Layer upon layer I added people and things to avoid. The list got longer and longer as I got older. Eventually I found myself overreacting to situations that didn't call for such a high level of emotion. I was even making the situations more complicated. My present reality was being polluted by the past. It was hard to distinguish between the two so I could keep them separate.

Then I wised up and took the time to get to the root of why I was having such strong reactions to various situations. I discovered the layers of emotions I'd buried were beginning to stink.

Friend, I pray that you will avoid the trap of burying your pain. It will always come back to haunt you. When people get upset, I no longer take their emotions and actions personally because now I know that if they're overreacting, it's because their past is rising to the surface. The current situation is merely an addition to the pile of unfinished business they are storing up.

When you think of conflict—major or minor—what comes to mind? I see a word said in haste, a miffed gesture, a certain look that sets off a chain reaction of alarms in the recipient's heart. She immediately goes into defense mode like an angry lioness protecting her cubs. Follow that with a kneejerk reaction from the first person to the second person, and soon a fire of emotions is raging out of control. In the aftermath of the disaster, everyone is wondering what happened and how the situation got so volatile.

Trust me on this one. I've learned from hard experience: *Every* piece of fruit comes from a root. All the unresolved issues that reach back as far as early childhood can impact our present reactions for good or bad. They might paralyze us or compel us to press past where we presently live to find higher, safer ground.

Women are so good at hiding disappointments and pain. Often we don't even know that we're prone to acting out the unresolved feelings. As I said earlier, years ago a young man told me I was beautiful. I'd not been told that before, and I thought I was ugly, so I reacted virulently, assuming he was making fun of me. Every time he said it, I got angry. I couldn't understand why he felt the need to keep lying to me.

Needless to say the relationship didn't go very far. After the breakup, a friend questioned my response and helped me realize my reaction was overkill. I soon recalled an incident when I was a child where someone called me ugly. The words had cut deep into my spirit and rested there, echoing through my mind and soul until it solidified into a fact instead of just one person's opinion. Passing comments can seem insignificant at the time, but often the feelings linger and fester. Feeling unlovely can lead to serious heart conditions such as envy, bitterness, and a critical spirit.

Perhaps if we took a moment to stop deflecting imagined or real insults and injuries, we might discover and lay past issues to rest. Then we could embrace the freedom that comes with coming out of hiding. As we allow the light of God to illuminate those dark, buried, hurting places in our hearts, what we truly thirst for will become clear—as well as the source for satisfying that need.

Reflections

1. *List the top three disappointments that come to mind for you right now.*

2. *What are your areas of struggle when it comes to reconciling these things?*

3. *What negative, kneejerk reactions have been borne from this?*

4. *When others tread close to these three areas, how do you react?*

5. *In what ways is it self-defeating for you not to deal with the things you've buried?*

Refreshing Streams

Nothing is lost in God's economy. Not even the fallout from mistakes and past failures can cause us to lose the blessings God has laid away for us. However, if we continue to ignore the negative thoughts and actions we store in our hearts, we may pay a dear price. Failed relationships, ill health, financial woes, difficulties in business, and so much more follow bitterness, envy, anger, and other results from negative emotions that have been allowed to fester. Let God take your hand and help you revisit the recesses of your heart. He will lovingly apply His healing touch so you will be released to experience new rivers of refreshing restoration. This fine surgery He performs reaches beyond the surface and goes directly to the wound, curing it and adjusting your heart to your new joyful reality. He cleanses you, heals you, and nurtures you back to life and right living. When you drink from His fountain, He will do what He does best—satisfy your deepest longings.

The purposes of a [woman's] heart are deep waters,
but a [woman] of understanding draws them out.
PROVERBS 20:5 NIV

Comparison Shopping

You are not greater than our father Jacob,
are You, who gave us the well, and
drank of it himself and his sons and his cattle?

❦

*I*t is inconceivable, she thought, *that anything better could exist.* As much as she didn't like the trek to the well, she was always spurred on by the refreshment that awaited her. At high noon the water seemed even colder and sweeter. *Is there any water better than this?* she wondered. It was hard to wrap her mind around the idea.

What if there really was something better? Would she be able to get it? She'd found that sometimes it was easier to settle for what was readily available. Why upset the status quo and leave herself open to frustration by focusing on the possibility that something better than what she already had existed? And yet she did wonder from time to time if this was all there is to life. The sameness of it was a subtle irritant, like an unscratchable itch at the back of her throat. She couldn't quite get to it. It was easier to ignore it and focus on something she could reach and pretend she wasn't missing out on anything. Call it sour grapes if you will, but in her mind it was about finding comfort wherever she could.

This stranger was slowly getting under her skin. He seemed familiar yet different. Just when she had relegated him to the ranks of all the other men who had approached her, he extended that strange offer. "Living water." What is living water? It sounded good. But was it that much better than what she already had? What was so different about his water?

She was used to making comparisons. She rated the men she had loved against the others. One was more romantic, another more generous, one more crude, another more faithful. A smile touched the corner of her lips as she revisited each man, one-by-one, focusing on the good traits. Then other memories cast a shadow across her face. She remembered they too had compared her to other women. How long her mind wandered down the long corridor of memories she couldn't say, but all of a sudden she was aware of the stranger still staring at her.

Is he debating whether he is greater than Jacob? she wondered. *Would he put himself on par with that great and successful patriarch?* The well Jacob had established was the center of village life. This was where everyone had gathered for as long as she could remember to draw water and visit. Everyone said the water was wonderful and satisfying. If there was better water somewhere perhaps it was a good thing she didn't know it. How horrible it would be to drink something wonderful and then have to return to the mediocre. That would be like giving your heart to a good man and then finding yourself alone again. Or never finding another man who could live up to what you had experienced before. She'd been there, done that. She'd concluded that everyone was destined to have an unrequited love that brought bittersweet memories of what once was and could never be again. Such was the unfairness of life.

So did this man really have access to "living water"? He seemed so confident. His demeanor made her even more curious. Though he seemed to be sure of himself, he didn't come across as thinking he was better than she was. He didn't talk down to her as if she were a slave or of no account. He seemed genuine in wanting to offer her something she had never tried. Something that would satisfy her longing in a way she'd never experienced.

Suddenly she realized that she believed him. That he had something to offer…and she wanted it.

I remember my first expensive pair of leather shoes. I had worked and saved to buy the Italian shoes that had captured my heart. There they sat in the window of a store I had never dared to venture into. In comparison to what I was used to, they were expensive…exclusive… beyond my reach. But one day those shoes beckoned. I had to have them. They haunted me, wearing me down until I was willing to pay the price. I remember entering the store and standing there until I felt I belonged inside. The salesman eyed me as if he were deciding if he should waste his time with me or not. I walked over to where the shoes were displayed. They were just as beautiful close up. I stood there in reverence, working up the nerve to ask if I could try them on.

"May I help you?" The salesperson's voice interrupted my reverie. I cleared my throat and asked if I could try them on. My voice sounded foreign to my ears. He asked what size, and I almost forgot what size I wore. He gave a courteous bow and went to retrieve the coveted shoes.

I panicked. My brain was saying to my feet, "This is your last chance to get away before he comes back with those shoes. What's wrong with you? You've never spent this kind of money on a pair of shoes in your life. Nothing is wrong with the shoes you've been wearing. What's the difference anyway? Manmade material and leather couldn't possibly be that different. And who do you think you are? What makes you think you deserve these fancy shoes? You could have three pairs of shoes for what you are about to pay for one."

"Here they are!" The salesman stood before me, shoes in hand. I could reach out and touch them. He motioned me to a seat. I sat on the edge watching him remove my right shoe and slide on the one he held in his hand. The coolness of the leather caressed my feet. He removed my other shoe and slid on the new one. I stood. I walked toward the mirror, ecstatic by the look and comfort of the shoes. I loved how they made me feel. I bought those shoes, and I've never looked back with an ounce of regret. And I've never looked at another pair of shoes that weren't well made and beautiful. The more I wore those shoes, the more convinced I became that I should have more of the same. They were wonderful. They molded to my feet, and my feet never hurt again. My feet now knew the difference between quality and "good enough to get by." Quality won.

Ignorance is bliss, people say. But I say it's not. Ignorance means you are being robbed. The Word of God says that people err and make bad mistakes because of lack of knowledge (Proverbs 10:14). What we don't know can and will hurt us eventually. Whether it is a better pair of shoes, a better deal on something we buy, a better job, a better home, a different mate, we all have longed for something better. We strive to be better people, and end up comparing ourselves to others, often to our detriment. I had to settle this issue with myself a long time ago because I was driving myself crazy. There will always be someone smarter, prettier, richer, thinner, shapelier, wittier…you name it. So all I can do is strive to be a better me. No one can do me like me.

But what about the things we long for deep in our core? Like a good, solid, happy marriage? A dream come true? A more secure existence? A really great job we can get excited about every day? So many people settle for less than the best. The general rule of thumb that seems to permeate our culture is that "something is better than nothing." We numb ourselves and convince ourselves that good is good enough. Some people fall prey to laziness, content to settle for what they have even if something better may be on the horizon. Others never quench their thirst for more. The expression on their faces says, "Is this all there is?"

Have you tried to satisfy yourself via your own efforts to no avail? Do you keep trying the same thing, over and over, expecting different results? As you review the outcomes of your choices, look to Jesus. He's stretching out His hands to you, signaling that He has something better for you.

The question becomes, "How thirsty are you?" Are you thirsty enough for change? Are you open to trying something new? The unknown can be scary, I know. But think what you might miss by not discovering all God has in store for you. Let go of the familiar and trust God to guide you. We all make choices that turn out to be pivotal, that propel us forward to a fascinating and fulfilling future. The secret is stepping out in faith. Nothing compares to the life and blessing God offers. Choose to drink living water from God's cup!

Reflections

1. *To whom have you compared yourself in the past? Why?*

2. *In what ways can you separate fact from fiction in your comparisons?*

3. *How do you get trapped in your comparisons?*

4. What makes you hesitant about new experiences?

5. What is the greatest challenge to getting past your present situation or mindset and moving forward in faith?

Refreshing Springs

God desires to take you from glory to glory. This implies from good, to great, to greater. Each level of living and loving in Him will transport you to a place better than the last. But you have a choice to make: to drink or not to drink from His cup. To drink and savor until He is ready to reveal another flavor or aspect of Himself. This is part of what makes the journey with God so exciting.

And each time you move with God, it isn't just a matter of whether something is better than what you had before. Most of the time it's whether something is better *for* you in the present moment. Understanding this will help you rest in where you are until you are presented with an invitation by God to experience an even greater revelation of what He has to offer. Jesus said He came that you "may have life, and have it abundantly" (John 10:10)!

Temporary Measures

*[Jesus said,] "Everyone who drinks of this water will
thirst again...But whoever drinks of the water that
I will give him shall never thirst."*

※

She had asked the man at the well if he was greater than Jacob, and His calm reply rocked her world. She understood about the well water. Obviously everyone got thirsty again. It was ludicrous to believe one drink of water could quench someone's thirst forever. People came to the well daily...sometimes several times a day...to draw yet again this liquid that refreshed and cleansed the body.

Deep in the recesses of her spirit she knew that the Jewish rabbi before her was speaking of more than physical water. His words suggested something much deeper. She thought of the moments of pleasure she'd snatched for herself here and there throughout her life.

Fleeting moments of gratification that never lasted. Shopping in the marketplace sometimes appeased her hunger for something more. As she swirled in front of the mirror in her new finery, she basked in the pleasure her reflection gave her in that moment. The joy in the new clothes would only last until the first washing. After that the garment would be old like all the others.

And then there were those moments when she bit into a guilty pleasure—a delicious dessert. The flavor satiated her. Suddenly life was a little more pleasant...until the last bite came and went. Then the hunger returned. She knew about filling up on things that would only temporarily satisfy. And the downward dip when the pleasure wore off seemed to be getting wider and deeper with each momentary spike of delight. The pain magnified her need—told her that something was missing, though she didn't know quite what it was.

Perhaps this stranger knows the answer, she thought. *He seems satisfied with life. He seems serene and confident. How does a person get to that place?* she wondered. She thought back on every time she'd thought she'd finally found happiness. Those times when life seemed to be lined up just the way she wanted it. It never lasted, and she felt the sands beneath her feet shifting like the tide that always returns the sea to the same level time and time again. She was always left wondering why she couldn't harness that feeling of satisfaction and keep it near.

What would it take to get to a place of consistent fulfillment that wouldn't wear off or be altered by what was happening around me? Is there such a place? She so badly wanted that. A place where she'd be happy and thrive instead of worrying about what was going to happen next and how she was going to survive.

She was beginning to realize that ultimately fulfillment had to do with mindset, with how she looked at things and viewed life. But that knowledge did nothing to abate her thirst. Nothing satisfied her deeply. Nothing settled the restlessness she felt. Like a bomb with a lit fuse, she knew an explosion was inevitable and her momentary contentment would go up in smoke. Her greatest fear was that of exercising the wrong impulse. She was afraid of what the unknown might cost her.

And here this man sat, suggesting she wasn't different than anyone else. That others were driven by a thirst they couldn't quench either. In one way it was nice to be considered "normal." To be considered the same as everyone else. And it was true. *Aren't we all creatures relegated to doing the best we can with what we've been given?* she mused. *Don't we all accept that nothing is permanent?* Even as she thought about the continual changes, she grew tired. A wave of exhaustion swept over her as she pondered that life would always be the same, an endless cycle of trying to get satisfied and find happiness, only to achieve them for a brief time before they're taken away. A moment of relief, another wave of thirst. A reprise from longing, and then even greater hunger. Did God realize their plight?

Did this Jewish man have an answer…a solution to the ups and downs? He was suggesting he did with his living water, but she couldn't conceive of never thirsting again. Never being so needy again. Was there rest for her soul? Hope surged and a river of relief washed over her. It would be wonderful to feel that way. Satisfied and content without interruption.

Did this man drink his living water? Is that why he looked so cool, so unruffled, so strong? Even at this hour when the sun was at its most brutal strength? Curiosity crept in.

She could feel the dryness of her soul longing for life-giving water.

Yes, I've said it, and I'm sure you've said it too. "If only I had this, my life would be complete. If only I could experience that I would finally be happy." Sadly, the fairy tales lied. There is no "happily ever after" on this side of eternity. There are moments of joy, glimpses of what it feels like to want for nothing. In those moments we catch fleeting reflections of heaven. But don't be fooled. Our completion will come only when we're physically with our Lord and Savior in His house, where He is preparing rooms for us (John 14:2-3). And when we're there, no doubts will cancel the pleasure of our time with Him. He will be right there before us! We'll be in His presence and full of joy.

The book of James says God can't be tempted (1:1). As I considered this, I found the realization of why this is very profound. In Him is the fullness of all things. All that He desires is already in Him. God is not full of Himself; He is full of *everything He has created.* They all abide, breathe, live, and have their very being in Him. He needs nothing outside of Himself because the source of all life lives in Him. He *is* the source!

God always was. And then He created the vast universe. Gene Edwards artfully writes in his book *The Divine Romance* that God folded Himself up and stepped inside the realm of the heavens and eternity and chose to dwell there. This suggests He was bigger than creation, eternity, and the heavens. Oh my!

God then creates man and woman for fellowship, though He already has the angels in place. He fills the earth with life and chooses to commune with His creatures on earth. When fellowship is broken between Him and the man and woman He created, He grieves. To restore the relationship, He asks His Son, Jesus, to be the needed sacrifice, an atonement so that mankind can once again commune freely with their Creator.

Jesus agrees and does precisely as God wants. Through Him we can approach God with the assurance that He loves us and cares about us. We lift our hearts and voices to Him in our worship, filled with His presence and joy. Although God is full and complete by Himself, with our worship we please Him.

Think of it this way. Have you ever overeaten a really good meal at a restaurant? About the time you were wondering if you could find a pin to pop your stomach to get some relief, the waiter appears with a desert tray laden with all your favorites. Much to your chagrin, and as much as you would like to choose one, you can't because you are too full. There is not one inch of room in your stomach for another bite no matter how good it might taste. And it may not taste that great because your taste buds are already satiated from all you've eaten already.

Well, God is full so He can't be tempted. And when He abides in us and we're one with Him, we too are full. Our joy is complete. We're filled with strength and possess His peace, which is beyond our earthly understanding. Outside circumstances can't rob us of what God has placed way down inside us. The world doesn't give us this deep fulfillment, and the world can't take it away. It's not contingent on who loves us, who doesn't love us, who understands us, who doesn't understand us, who fails to accept us. Our significance is based on our relationship with our Creator. And when we accept this in our hearts, we are flooded with His everlasting love.

This is a foreign concept for those who continue to grasp at straws, to seek happiness and contentment on an earthly level. The sparks of gratification they find leave greater voids in their hearts and souls. Pleasure seeking leads to dangerous games of intensified scrapping to find greater excitement, more outrageous highs, and amazing thrills. The hole in all our hearts has nothing to do with earthly relationships, experiences, or accomplishments. Failing to understand this has everything to do with unrelenting thirst. Refreshing relief only comes when we stop the chase for what doesn't satisfy and fall into the arms of the One who wants to cool our fevered brows and soothe our parched souls.

God wants us to be complete, fulfilled, saturated with satisfaction even more than we long for it. Why? Because He loves us more than we can understand. He wants His beauty, love, power, and wisdom to fill us and then flow through us to the people around us.

Dare to be surprised by joy. Fling yourself into the loving arms of your Savior and Lord. Bathe in the living water that cleanses and restores and brings greater life. Drink deep.

Reflections

1. Where have you been seeking satisfaction?

2. *In what ways are you left wanting from this?*

3. *What was your expectation of the situation or relationship?*

4. *In what ways have your expectations been part of the problem?*

5. *What can you do to avoid disappointment next time?*

Refreshing Springs

When you set the ground rules for what will make you happy, you are destined to fall short of your goal. Human imagination plays tricks on your heart and mind, leading you down paths of frustration on the way to goals that can't be realized. It paints pictures of an oasis boasting of the ultimate experience, but it delivers only a shadow of what was promised. And then you stand gazing at the emptiness, wondering why the peace and joy you desire continues to elude you. That is where God meets you and offers His love and strength and insights to illuminate your understanding. And the more you release your desires and expectations to Him, the greater your blessings in return. God always delivers. He is the God of abundance! He'll supply your needs *and* your wants as you follow His wonderful plans for you. He wants you fulfilled, and He wants you to be whole.

> *"I know the plans that I have for you," declares the LORD,*
> *"plans for welfare and not for calamity*
> *to give you a future and a hope."*
> JEREMIAH 29:11

PART 3

What Do You Want?

Is it hard to chart a path toward where you want to go because you're not clear on where you are? If you call any transportation help center for directions, the first question the help desk person will ask is, "Where are you now?" You have to be able to say where you are now and give a specific location for your destination. And you have to know where you're going so you can focus on what you need for the journey and the manner in which you will travel.

I've noticed that a lot of people go around in circles, arriving back at the same place again and again. I've been guilty of this myself. Ending up back where I started is a great disappointment. We get glimpses of what might be a great destination or experience to answer the cries of our hearts, but we usually miss the turn because we haven't identified our core needs. Searching for what is visible rarely encourages us to deal with the root of the problem that lies beneath, to figure out why we aren't finding the joy we seek.

Most people caught in a cycle of disappointment rarely get to the crux of why they're going in circles. They often blame others or their situation to displace the responsibility for not attaining their goals. They are crying out for a fix without knowing what truly needs to take place for lasting change and fulfillment to occur.

The woman at the well thought the living water Jesus spoke of would be the answer to her problem because it would keep her from being thirsty, meaning she wouldn't have to face the townspeople's disapproval on the way to the well. These were surface issues in her life. They weren't her true need, her heart need. She needed a Savior. She needed a true worship experience where she engaged with God on a personal level. But that seemed out of reach so she focused on getting an immediate, temporary fix.

We all get distracted by such "low-hanging fruit." And if we don't know what we really need, we will seek only the obvious and seemingly immediate fix. The danger is that we might become content with this when God has so much more for us. We need to find what will ultimately sustain us even when the environment of our lives is swirling with temptations to try what can't really satisfy.

At the core of our souls are very basic identity questions:

- Who am I?
- What do I value most?
- What is my reason for getting up every morning?
- What do I want my life to look like to me? To God? To others?
- What do I want my legacy to be?
- What mark do I want to leave on the hearts of people I encounter?
- What will give me peace and fulfillment?
- What do I want—really want?

When we focus on these questions and work toward the answers, our goals and achievements will begin to line up with these foundational markers. Our choices will radiate around these basic spokes and drive most of the moves we make. If we ignore these questions or only give them surface consideration, we'll become directionless, falling for false promises of joy and chasing rainbows in hopes of finding gold. Our lives will become pointless and constant searches for the impossible.

Every decision we make should reflect the direction we want to go in life. So many distractions abound to get us off course from our core desires and passions that we need to be on guard against them. Perhaps this is why God said to write the vision and make it plain so that we can run with it (Habakkuk 2:2). The key to winning the race is focus and a clear sense of where the finish line lies.

Maps are beautiful. They help us get to our destination if we follow the route that is charted. I love my global positioning satellite gadget! What did people do before GPS? We got lost, that's what we did! There are so many spiritual principles that can be taught based on our interactions with the little lady or little man that talks to us from that little box. For instance, sometimes I don't trust the lady in my GPS. I question the route she wants me to take. Instead of following her instructions, I go the way I want to. This is often the way I already know. Then I end up stuck in traffic. That is when I realize the GPS had considered the route and directed me on an alternate course to help me avoid traffic delays. Spiritually speaking, I've learned that sometimes I'm the greatest source of delay and disappointment in my life because I've not listened to or followed God's directions.

God knows what we want more than we do. His Holy Spirit searches our hearts and makes intercession for us in accordance with God's will. That prayer invites God's instruction and intervention into our lives. And when we follow His voice, we will arrive at our destination energized and strengthened by the journey.

Sometimes our ability to pinpoint our needs can be accomplished only by coming to the end of ourselves, by finally realizing all the things we've tried haven't worked. Liberation is found by no longer insisting on our own way. We lay down our pride and confess what isn't working. Then God, who honors repentance and humility, draws close because we're getting real with ourselves and with Him, confessing the truth of what we've wrought on our own. He doesn't laugh, sneer, or judge our failed attempts. He focuses on our restoration and reconciliation to our relationship with Him and shows us His path that will get us to our goal. He is more determined for us to be blessed than we are to claim the blessing. Why? Because when we are liberated and victorious He is glorified.

When we avoid God's simple path, we can veer onto a route that leads us further away from our hearts' desires. The insistence on being the captain of our own ships and making vows of "I won't do this" for self-protection usually lead us nowhere fast. And sometimes our self-protection mode keeps us from the very thing we want.

God tells us to be careful not to make vows lest we break them and destroy the work of our hands (Ecclesiastes 4:4-6). Vows are usually spoken rashly: "I'll never let that happen again." "That's the last time I'll allow someone to hurt me." "I'll never fall in love again." Now we know the person who says she'll never fall in love again desperately wants to experience love. But because of her vow, anyone who reaches out to her will be repelled by her fear and wariness. Her shields and defenses are up as she waits for an invitation to love that will keep her heart safe. That moment will never come because human love is always a risk.

Jesus came to earth knowing He would be rejected by some. He was willing to endure the pain of watching people turn away from His love. He knew what He wanted to do—save as many people as would believe in His name (John 1:11). He focused on the goal and gave Himself to redeem us. Despising the shame, He focused on the joy set before Him—us. We were the prize, and in His mind we were worth dying for. He remained vulnerable. He was misinterpreted and misrepresented. He was insulted, rejected, reviled, lied about, betrayed, and eventually crucified. None of this made Him draw back from His mission to claim us as His bride. He counted the cost and prepared Himself for all that would come against Him, forging through moments of agony and despair. He stayed on task, allowing everything nonessential to fall away like water off a duck's back. He refused to be deterred by irrelevant side trips. When we know what we want, we also realize what might not be important.

So are we really protecting our sanity and hearts when we make "I will never" vows? Or are we limiting ourselves and closing ourselves off to possible benefits and positive experiences? Vows generally create harsh boundaries that few people want to live within very long. "Never say never" is a popular adage...and it's true. We never know where life will take us. Endless possibilities await us in God's plans.

Vows are smokescreens, seemingly safe distractions from the truth and the anticipated pain of facing it. Shutting down emotionally and not paying attention to what we truly need doesn't ensure peace or happiness because the Spirit of God within us knows better. His gentle prompting will continue until it seems to reverberate and drown out all else, including the din of rationalizations.

And don't believe the deception that we don't or can't miss what we've never had or acknowledged that we want. That's just not true. The desires God gives us remain whether we pay attention to them or not. They sit in the pit of our guts letting us know something is missing. God is saying, "I want this for you!" You can walk away, hoping you're protecting yourself against disappointment, but the Holy Spirit will continue to prompt you. Fearfully pulling back from the truth hinders your relationship with God. I encourage you to take a deep breath, turn to God, confess your fears, and ask Him to help you.

"Lord, here is my need. Please take it and fulfill it for me." This is when God does some of His best work. He takes our confessed needs and desires and turns them into something beautiful. Something good and perfect that blesses you *and* others. My philosophy is to take the things I moaned about during the testing time and make them a testimony to the Lord. Squeeze them for all they are worth and find the lessons and joy. You'll also find freedom in being true to yourself and true to God. There is no shame in confessing your sins and errors and needs; it opens portals that lead to freedom, hope, and peace.

9

Irresistible Offers

*Sir, give me this water,
so I will not be thirsty nor
come all the way here to draw [water].*

❧

The sun was getting hotter, her throat was getting drier by the minute. The more the stranger spoke of this living water, the thirstier she got. She was always thirsty, it seemed. Nothing quenched her desire for water, for love, for peace, for anything. She sometimes wondered what was wrong with her. Why couldn't she ever be satisfied? Had she missed something along the way? Was there a flaw in her character? Or was there something more she just hadn't discovered yet? Was it possible to actually not thirst?

And if she never thirsted again, she wouldn't have to take this walk of shame through town every day to get to the well. That would be almost heavenly. No more stares, no more whispers, no more cruel words. Perhaps she could finally find some measure of peace within herself. If she didn't have to constantly deal with the negative judgments of others, she might be better able to accept her lot in life.

She knew her life didn't measure up in the eyes of others, but she was doing the best she could. Why would people blame her for doing what she needed to survive? And yet they did. The women shunned her. The men were careful when others were around. You could cut the air with a knife whenever she appeared in public. The silence followed by murmurs were suffocating. Though she held her head high, inwardly she crumpled. She was sick of the condemnation, of her discomfort, of the same routine day in and day out. She was tired of the repeat cycle of her lifestyle. It was like cleaning house. She'd get it done but then have to do it again the next day. Moving forward but not really going anywhere. Finding herself back in the same place. This well offered a temporary respite at best. If only she didn't have to come to this place. If only she could stop being so thirsty.

Yes, this living water might be the solution. If she could get this water the Jewish man spoke of, she would no longer be subjected to feelings of disgrace or incessant thirst. She felt like the dogs she saw panting on the side of the road. She just wanted to breathe freely.

"Sir, give me this water, so I will not be thirsty nor come all the way here to draw [water]," she blurted. The words were out before she had time to modulate her voice into one of cautious interest. She felt naked in her own admission. She cast her gaze downward, afraid her eyes would betray the hope that swelled in her heart. He didn't need to know all her business, just that she was interested in what he had to offer.

This man was the first person to look at her devoid of a hidden agenda. He didn't want anything from her; he seemed to be interested in her welfare. His care felt comforting and yet foreign. It was the unknown that made her keep her guard up. He was a stranger after all, and she had to keep reminding herself of that to keep from getting too comfortable.

What would it be like to be free of the burden of longing? To be free from taking the lonely journey to the well day in and day out? That sounded so good…so refreshing. Again her gaze went to the stranger who was considering her words. His expression told her he wasn't taking her request lightly. Again she warmed to the thought of being taken seriously. Of being significant. Of being validated by his attention. She felt like a light had been turned on in her soul. She wanted to feel that way all the time. Was that too much to hope for?

In the desert seasons of my life I've surveyed the terrain of vast nothingness before me and asked, "Is this all there is?" Trudging through the sameness of days that stretch before me without a sign that anything new is about to occur, I feel parched by disappointment and long for something different. Something to rock the status quo. Something that will give me a sign that a breakthrough is on the way. "How long around this mountain, Lord?" I ask. Usually in those moments I get no answer. I keep pushing forward, one foot in front of the other, hoping for a bend in the road. For rain. For a passing cloud. For a whisper in the wind. Something…anything. An assurance that things will get better. That this is not all there is. That God has not forgotten me. That He will come through for me.

I'm embarrassed in those moments when I feel I've failed. When my affairs aren't pristinely arranged in a way that garners approval from my family, friends, and observers. I've hung my head in shame as I was asked, "How could you make that choice?" "What are you going to do now?" "Did you consider the facts and the situation before plunging in?" As I answer each question with a shrug, nothing changes. There is that look and that silence that says it all. At least in my mind I hear the condemnation. Granted, my own issues and views might be coloring how I perceive their questions and reactions.

When I am unable to solve my dilemmas in record time, I begin to see people's concern as a ruler measuring my progress—or lack of progress. Their questions become interrogations I don't want to face or endure. I want to hide until everything is back on track. Until improvements have been made. Movement forward has been accomplished so they'll smile and offer me their approval once again. Until then I feel defeated, stupid, and uncomfortable. And it's even worse when the mistakes and failures are repeated. I'm sure you know what I'm talking about. When we're at that place we question our abilities, our decisions, our faith, and more. We purpose to do better next time and say, "Lord, if You get me out of this place, I won't come back here again."

Do you have your own "well" you travel to time and again, longing for relief? You have a love/hate relationship with yourself and the things you reach for because they don't satisfy you. And often they enlarge the gaping nothingness your soul feels in those moments. At other times the nothingness feels familiar—not fulfilling but better than some of the alternatives and far less scary than the unknown.

Still God waits for us to seek Him in our troubles. He waits for us to get to the end of ourselves and realize our attempts to prop up our lives, fix our messes, make things happen, and satisfy ourselves are failing. God uses our weariness and disappointment to motivate us to open our hearts to something new. Yes, unfortunately sometimes it is our dryness and desperation that drives us to our knees with open palms, saying, "Have Your way, Lord!" Out of energy, drive, determination, and answers, we finally land at the foot of the cross drenched in tears of frustration, finished with our attempts to fix ourselves and our circumstances.

"Stick a fork in me, I'm done." I've said this on more than one occasion. I believe God gets so excited when I say that. "I give up!" is another one of my lines He enjoys. Finally I am out of the way, stepping aside, listening for His guidance, and then moving forward with Him. Living streams of water are flowing at last. Think of it this way: No one appreciates a cold drink like some who is parched and dying. As we hold out open hands before God He comes bearing not just a drink—but *rivers* of renewal. Streams of living water to wash away the present pain and provide an endless supply of soul-refreshing love.

Reflections

1. *What do you thirst for?*

2. *What has been or is your "well" that never satisfies?*

3. *What have been your expectations in this situation?*

4. *What was your response when you were disappointed or unfulfilled?*

5. *What place do you not want to return to?*

Refreshing Springs

One thing you must accept in your life is the inevitable seasons. However some seasons are of your own creation and others are allowed by God for your growth. In no way does God want you to adopt a victim mentality. Jesus said that He has come that you might have life abundantly. This implies that you are to have life. Life and the circumstances that arise are not to rule you. There is no such thing as being stuck when you're in Christ. He

has equipped you to rise above your issues and circumstances and glorify Him as you overcome. In the midst
of all your setbacks He remains faithful to His promises
to deliver you!

> *The faithful love of the Lord never ends!*
> *His mercies never cease.*
> *Great is his faithfulness; his mercies be-*
> *gin afresh each morning.*
> LAMENTATIONS 3:22-23 NLT

10

The Truth

[Jesus] said to her, "Go, call
your husband and come here."
The woman answered,
"I have no husband."

🦅

Whe hen the rabbi told her to go get her husband it was like a knife
pierced the Samaritan woman's heart. *Does he know what he's*
asking? It was a harmless assumption that she was married. She was certainly old enough. And she *had been* married. Discomfort squeezed
the breath from her lungs. *How should I answer him?* How could she
couch the uncomfortable truth of her situation so it didn't sound so
bad? She didn't want to face his disapproval. She had so enjoyed being
in the presence of nonjudgmental company. Would he think less of her
if he knew the truth? Though she'd suffered at the hands of her family,

neighbors, and associates, she'd learned to block out their opinions. She had to do what she had to do.

This was her life. She'd made the necessary adjustments to move forward. It wasn't the most ideal situation, but it was satisfactory for now. But she didn't want to talk about it. She kept her business to herself. She didn't discuss the details of her relationship with anyone, much less a stranger.

How could she get what she wanted without opening the door and exposing her lifestyle? Her insides churned. She suddenly took a good hard look at the road she'd chosen for herself and what that meant for her life. She stood rooted to the spot. The lump in her throat growing larger, strangling the answer rising in her throat. She wasn't sure how much time passed before she got the words out. He was waiting... waiting...waiting. His eyes showed no guile or sinister agenda. They were clear and filled with compassionate interest.

"I have no husband," she finally said. "No husband." The words echoed in the silence. *Did I just lie?* she wondered. She wasn't sure. Well, perhaps it was half a lie. She left out the living with a man part. But her statement was true. She didn't have a husband.

The truth sunk in. It was as if someone had yanked the scab off a long-festering wound. Though it had been buried under layers of thick skin that kept comments at bay, the pain was still there, laid bare, raw, infected. She bit her bottom lip. She hadn't realized until that moment how deep the hurt still went. She struggled to keep back the tears. She pressed her lips together to keep from exposing anything more. Now it was her turn to wait.

⁂

I recall being so in love with a man once I could hardly stand it. The trouble was that he wasn't in love with me. I played games with him and me. Every bit of attention he gave me, no matter how small, I took as a sign that he had feelings for me. My friends tried to rein in my attitude and behavior as they gently told me the truth, but to no avail. I didn't want to hear it. I refused to hear it. I wanted what I wanted.

Yes, he thought I was nice, but he didn't love me. He didn't want me that way. I couldn't receive or accept this. As time went by and waiting for him to realize what I already believed went past my heart's deadline, the pain finally forced me to confront him. "Are you ever going to marry me?" I asked. Without blinking or hesitating, he looked me straight in the eye and said, "No, Michelle. I am never going to marry you."

My entire world crumpled before my eyes. The pain was excruciating. I wanted to die. And yet, deep down inside, I had already known the truth. I'd just refused to face it.

The truth can hurt. It can cut deep, slicing our strength into shreds and threatening to chop our hearts into little bits. Even though we might not realize it, this is when we are able to really breathe. Even if we don't like the truth, it still will set us free…free to move on. Denial is bondage. We can't move forward if we're stuck in "where we wish we were." We need to acknowledge fully where we are and then move past it. Accept the pain as the attention getter it is. Let it burn going down, removing anything that impairs our vision from seeing the situation as God sees it. Although it hurts, it's a "good" hurt because it is helping us grow and embrace change.

Pain is best treated as a friend. I remind myself of this often. God gave us the ability to feel pain because it lets us know there's a problem, and it forces us to deal with what is wrong or what we've buried, overlooked, or refused to surrender to God. When we stop and listen to the hurt, we uncover secrets our deceptive hearts may have believed or perpetrated. Jeremiah 17:9 says, "The heart is more deceitful than all else."

God stands patiently, waiting for us to open our hands to show Him our hearts so He can do what He does best—pour on the oil of love and forgiveness and heal us. So often He says, "Give me your pain," and we reply, "What pain? I don't have any pain." Our denial keeps us slaves to the very thing we want to be rescued from. We don't want to go there because change might be required. You see, admission or exposure of the truth bears great responsibility.

"What are you going to do about it?" That's the next question I

don't like to hear. I say, "I don't like how this relationship is going." And
God says, "What are you going to do about it?" We want to check out
the alternatives for getting the life, the love, the circumstances we want
before giving up what we have. But the walk of faith doesn't always expose those options until we face the truth and surrender to the will of
God.

Sometimes God simply says, *"I know the plans I have for you."*

And we say, "What plans might those be exactly? I'd like to know
if it's going to be better than what I've been clinging to. Even though I
don't like it, at least I know what it is."

And God says, *"I have plans for you—for good and not for evil."*

And we reply, "Well, that's just too vague, God. Can you be more
specific?"

And the conversation continues until our pain forces us to scream
the truth: "My choices and decisions aren't working!" There we've finally
said it. When we turn to God and open our tear-stained hands and say,
"God, look at the mess I've made," He gently extricates what we're holding and makes it right. That's all God wants. For us to be honest with
Him and with ourselves. "'Come now, and let us reason together,' says
the LORD, 'though your sins are as scarlet, they will be as white as snow'"
(Isaiah 1:18). Just in case we are afraid of the work it's going to take to
fix our situation, God offers to do the hardest part for us. He cleanses
us and then empowers and encourages us to cooperate with His restoration plan.

Acknowledging the truth about where we are and where we'd like
to be is the beginning of the route to freedom. Acknowledging both
of these illuminates the path to get to the other side of our situations.
The truth is our guide, noting where we want to go, where we are now,
and calculating the best route to arrive at our desired destinations. But
it can't do that without first knowing where we are. When we grow
weary of our location personally, spiritually, financially, professionally,
or emotionally, we can let our exhaustion give way to the truth instead
of making excuses for staying where we are. Don't wait until life stares
you in the eyes and asks for what you don't have. Take a deep breath,

exhale, and talk to God today…right now. Tell Him the truth and ask for His help.

Reflections

1. *What is the truth about your current situation?*

2. *Are you having difficulty embracing or confessing this truth?*

3. *What needs to happen so you will face the truth and do something different this time?*

4. *What coping strategies are no longer working for you?*

5. *What are you going to do about that?*

Refreshing Streams

Have you heard the saying, "God can't fix what you won't admit"? Aye, there's the rub. The truth can be painful, and yet God insists on it. He calls you to come and reason with Him. Though your sins be as scarlet, He will make them white as snow. You can't do it. You can't make yourself clean. But when you ask, the Lord washes you with His Word and His love and His truth. He is faithful to forgive if you will be brave enough to confess your failings.

He loves to work with honest people. He wants to do away with your pride that denies your undone state and makes excuses and justifications for it. Oh that you will be brave enough to look in the mirror and see yourself as you truly are and acknowledge it. In that moment Jesus becomes your present help in time of need. He extends His grace to cool your fevered soul. His mercy is like liquid, filling all the gaps and crevices so you are completely refreshed and renewed.

11

Quiet As It's Kept

*Jesus said to her, "You have correctly said,
'I have no husband'; for you have had five husbands,
and the one whom you now have is not your husband;
this you have said truly."*

She gasped as his words pierced her. How did he know that? She felt naked. She searched his eyes for condemnation or disgust. There was no judgment in his expression—just compassion. His eyes still seemed warm and inviting.

She was confused. If he knew all of this about her, why didn't he judge her. Why was he talking to her so politely? But even as she asked herself this question her thoughts were being propelled back…back… back to her first love. She'd thought it would be a forever love. And then one day it ended. She was devastated. Every tomorrow looked emptier than the first. The pain squeezed the life out of her. Her eyes became empty, seeing nothing but loss. It was all she could do to crawl out of bed in the morning. There was no life without the man she loved. Food tasted like sand. The flavor was gone. The tears she cried seemed endless until finally she had none left. She was spent, poured out like a thin stream of liquid on a blazing fire. She couldn't be comforted. She would never love again, never laugh again, never live again.

And then it happened. She *did* love again. There was the euphoria of surprise that she was able to find love once again. And then it ended too. He was gone, taking her restoration with him. She wondered why fate had repeated this in her life. Caught between the fear of loving and the fear of living alone, she dared to embrace yet another man, but this time she was more careful. Just about the time she relaxed and dared to breathe, he too was gone. And still she hungered for love. She accepted another man but never lost the fear that he would leave. And he did.

She drew the curtains over her heart, refusing to invest what was left. She went through the motions of life without the emotions. She realized that in some cases it wasn't the men she missed. No, it was the pieces of herself she'd given away that could never be retrieved. After her last husband departed, she made a silent vow. She would stop hurting, stop hoping, stop being a fool. There were no guarantees in love. She would never let her guard down again. No more commitments that could be broken. She would only let a man come so far into her world. She would anticipate and expect nothing.

Nothing...and yet she longed for so much more.

How simple life had been when she dreamed little girl dreams of love that lasted. Of powerful men who saved her from pain and at times even herself. A once-in-a-lifetime love that would make her happy all of her days. But that hadn't happened. The love cycle turned out to be a source of pain, a source of shame. When she was willing to admit it, she acknowledged that at times the shame was greater than the pain.

As time went on, there were other men in her life. Though the people in her community didn't know all the details of the break-ups, they all gossiped and asked each other, "What is she doing with all these men?" Those without love cast envious judgments against her. Those who were married held their husbands closer as they watched her go by, anxiously glancing to see if their partners' gazes were wandering and lingering too long on her. She was competition.

Caught up in a war that raged around her, she was not out to steal anyone's man. She just wanted to find comfort and security. She shouldn't have to and wouldn't apologize for being beautiful. After all, the married women were in their cozy homes, safe and secure, while she struggled to maintain her existence. No, she would not apologize or allow their opinions to make her question herself.

Yes, she had made many vows to protect her heart. She could envision the wall around her heart growing thicker, digging deeper into the foundation of her core. She wondered what was on the other side but was too afraid to venture from behind its protection. So she had settled in with her current man. If they lived together maybe he wouldn't leave. She refused to get her hopes up for a more permanent relationship so she wouldn't get hurt again. Yes, it was a safe but lonely prison. It was familiar; she knew every nook and cranny. There would be no surprises, and that was good enough for her.

At least it had been until this stranger seemed to suggest that "good enough" was just another name for a place called "wanting."

❦

We have a tendency to make vows that hem us in behind and before as we try to control our circumstances. Before long we wonder how we got to this place where we've set ourselves up to repel the intimacy we long for. Vows can be severe prisons. They are hard to break through, and the longer we cling to our resolve the harder it becomes to leave. So we find justifications for why we are where we are. Initially they sound very good. Until someone comes along and shows us what we're missing. Or the loneliness or pain gets too great and we turn to God, who runs down the list of what led us to this place and our fear, pain and hurt are exposed again. The sensitive roots quiver and recoil from the possibility of further damage. If we let Him, Jesus will take our wounds and bind them up with His healing balm and love so they heal without leaving lasting scars.

This reminds me of the day I took my dog Matisse for a walk. He was happy to be out in the open air, and he was even happier when he saw his buddy Cooper, a Wheaton Terrier, waiting for him at the doggy park. In his excitement he ran to the fence to greet his furry friend. Cooper was just as elated to see Matisse, so excited in fact that he promptly lifted his leg and sprayed my little dog. Matisse took a step back and looked at Cooper in dismay, shook himself, and then went back to greeting his overly excited friend. After a towel down, I thought everything was okay. But every dog we encountered wanted to "baptize" Matisse again. I couldn't figure out what was happening until I realized they were attracted to the scent that still lingered on Matisse's fur. Obviously my towel had not done the job. The issue was deeper. When we got back home I put him in the sink for a good shampooing. While washing him, I reflected on the lingering odor.

In my life I haven't been so quick to recover when someone "rains on my parade," so to speak. I sit and stew and marinate in the situation for a while. The offense sinks into my pores, and I carry the lingering stench of anger, sadness, and irritation without being aware that it's showing in my actions and attitudes. Only when I take the situation to Jesus and allow Him to wash me, cleansing beneath the layers of built-up hurts, that the pattern is halted and broken.

Sadly, the scent of unreleased disappointment, offense, rejection, betrayal, and so on has a tendency to attract more of the same. The more it attracts similar states, the more we begin to align mentally, spiritually, and emotionally with our bad experiences, thereby attracting even more of the very things we fear. We perpetuate our pain until we are so overwhelmed that we try to escape by deciding not to feel anymore. We are left with only the memories of simpler times when it was fun to be naïve and open and see where life took us.

As we take our more defensive and tentative steps, measuring each one and looking for cracks to avoid, we get caught in a joyless existence. Our souls dry up, and we're consumed by the dust of resignation.

Then one day a Stranger comes and asks us for a drink, and then invites us to drink from His living water. As our dry and weary hearts long for relief, we contemplate this Man's special offer and long to accept His invitation. What about you? Will you decide that accepting the refreshment is more frightening than remaining in the dry and painful reality of where you are? Or will you reach out in faith and accept the life-giving elixir of God's love and favor offered through His Son Jesus Christ?

Reflections

1. *What cycles of setbacks have occurred in your life?*

2. *How do you handle setbacks?*

3. *Have you made vows to protect yourself? If yes, what have they been?*

4. *In what way have those vows imprisoned you or hurt you in the long run?*

5. *What do you long for but are afraid to openly hope for?*

Refreshing Springs

David put it beautifully in Psalm 42. His soul searched for God in a dry and weary land. He panted like a deer pants for refreshing water. Is your soul dry? Are you panting for the very things that will make your soul even more dry?

I believe Jesus' message to the woman at the well was clear to her when He reminded her of her romance history: "Six men and you are still thirsty. You are looking for life in the wrong places. No man, no possession, no achievement will truly satisfy your heart. Though you do gain in some ways, you remain thirsty or will soon thirst again." You need living water from your Savior and Lord. With His water comes hope—hope for tomorrow, no matter what has already transpired. When you stop insisting on finding other means of satisfaction and drink deeply from God's Spirit, you'll discover peace, refreshment, and joy.

PART 4

What Is Worship?

Paul urged Christians, "Present your bodies a living and holy sacrifice, acceptable to God, which is your spiritual service of worship" (Romans 12:1-2). People in today's churches often joke that "the only problem with a living sacrifice is that it keeps crawling off the altar." I wonder how many people have a clear understanding of worship. Like the Samaritan woman at the well who said that her people worshiped God on a mountain, a lot of people feel that worship is relegated to a specific place—a church, for example.

Jesus clarifies that when we know *who* we worship, we will understand that worship can't be contained. It surrounds our everyday living experience. It encompasses every aspect of our lives. Worship isn't relegated to a Sunday morning service with 20 minutes of music and song. Worship is a 24/7 experience! Every minute of every day we are to walk out the truth of God and live in obedience to His Word and His principles. The highest form of worship is obedience.

The trick of "religion" is to make worship an ethereal experience that is separate from the rudiments of everyday life. But this is not what God had in mind. If all creation worships God in its very existence, how much more should we? Perhaps that doesn't sound glamorous enough from a religion aspect, but *worship is not about us.* It is about what brings pleasure to our sovereign God. Worship is not something we do; it is what we are.

The woman at the well told Jesus, "Sir, I perceive that You are a prophet" (John 4:19). In His reply, Jesus said,

> Woman, believe Me, an hour is coming when neither in this mountain nor in Jerusalem will you worship the Father. You worship what you do not know; we worship what we know, for salvation is from the Jews. But an hour is coming, and now is, when the true worshipers will worship the Father in spirit and truth; for such people the Father seeks to be His worshipers. God is spirit, and those who worship Him must worship in spirit and truth (John 4:21-25).

This was what befuddled the woman at the well. Jesus was telling her she didn't understand worship because she didn't know *who* she was worshiping. She didn't know what God desired because there had been no exchange between them to give her this knowledge. She didn't have a personal relationship with God. Perhaps she didn't realize that, like a friend who knows the list of your favorites and knows what to do to bring a smile to your face, people were created for God's pleasure.

The enemy of our souls knows this too. As part of his unrelenting crusade to usurp God, one of Satan's revenge tactics is to steal worship from God. The devil's game plan? To hurt and interfere with us to the point that our worship of God shuts down, subsequently grieving God's heart. As we lie in the ruins of our rebellion, Satan laughs all the way down his slippery path, his work done. To pinpoint the foundations of worship and dismantle our enemy's strategy, we need only look to where he attacks.

Praise

First Satan attacks our desire to praise God. He knows God loves to receive our offerings of praise and thanksgiving. And he knows that praising and worshiping God strengthens us and makes His reality more present and real to us. Worship reminds us of the power and splendor of God—of His omniscience. But most important, worship reminds us that God *reigns* over all things. No problem is too big for Him to handle. As long as we magnify God, all that we wrestle with is diminished. But the moment we magnify our problems, we will be overwhelmed by fear and doubt.

Sometimes I wrestle with whether God can really do anything about my situation. Can you relate? By worshiping God, we solidify His majesty in our minds and remind ourselves of who He is. This knowledge helps our faith and enables us to stand firm for Him in the midst of trials.

Giving to God

The next area Satan likes to attack is our giving, which is also an area of worship. God loves cheerful givers. Money is one of the greatest arenas for warfare in the lives of believers. Today the battle to stay free of debt is at an all-time high as we wrestle with the cost of living, out-of-control spending habits, sudden financial setbacks, job losses, unexpected intrusions on our budgets, and the temptation of easy credit. The emergencies of life eat away at our nest eggs—if we've managed to accumulate any.

When we feel we can't get what we need or meet our needs, fear steps in and we question whether we should be giving to the church or mission work. Lack promotes fear of giving. When our needs begin to dominate our thoughts, we rationalize that God can wait for His offerings. We justify not giving to others in need because we are weathering our own financial storms. Or sometimes we just get distracted by the pleasure of having money and all the things it lets us buy. This can lead to an emphasis on possessions, which can lead to greed and materialism, which bends our hearts away from the One who gives us the power to gain wealth.

Worship includes the simple (but not always easy!) acts of saying no to our flesh and yes to the Holy Spirit. It can be as simple as not telling off someone who has deliberately offended us. Choosing to pursue God's peace and flee from strife is worship because it's exhibiting the fruit of the Spirit. Operating in love. Taking the high road. Avoiding giving into our lower nature. These are forms of worship when not done in an attempt to gain brownie points or privileges or perks from God. They can be our way of showing gratitude for what He has already done for us by sacrificing His Son Jesus for our redemption. He ransomed us from death and hell!

Let's be careful to not embrace the spirit of entitlement and be deceived into believing God owes us more. If He never did another thing for any of us, He's already done more than enough by His one divine act of kindness in arranging for our salvation. Our loving obedience can be one of the greatest ways we have to thank God. And even then God chooses to reward our obedience by fulfilling the promises He's made to us when we follow His commands.

Like any good parent who rewards their children with good things when pleased, our heavenly Father loves to give wonderful gifts to us. And they are gifts because there is nothing we can do to repay Him for enabling us to come to Him through Jesus. Salvation is a completely free gift He chooses to give us, and the other blessings He bestows on us are His unmerited favor at work in our lives because of His great love.

Sexual Intimacy

This area isn't discussed very often as a form of worship. But if we're looking at what Satan attacks and tries to pervert in the lives of believers, we have to look at this aspect as well. Sexual intimacy within marriage is beautiful in God's eyes. He created our ability to experience sexual pleasure and established marriage as a protective, secure place for sexual intimacy to enhance our lives and help us procreate.

This special, divinely inspired act of intimacy has been attacked at every angle by the powers of hell. Single people living committed lives for Christ struggle with staying celibate. The world throws so many sensual images at everyone these days that many societies question whether God's standards of purity and His emphasis on marriage before having a sexual relationship is that important, a big deal, or even within the realm of possibility. But if sex wasn't a big deal, Satan wouldn't attack the marriage bed as much as he does. Think about it. We wait with bated breath to get married so we can have sex. And then once we're married sex gets entangled with emotions and needs and couples often fail to come together as they should for mutual satisfaction. Then adultery runs rampant. And then there are the sexual practices that grieve the heart of God and violate the sanctity of intimacy.

Why would Satan wage such a serious attack against marriage and sexuality if it weren't important to God? What is sex? What is worship? They are both acts of giving all we have and are to the ones we love. It is being naked and unashamed before our beloveds. Holding nothing back. Becoming one. Just as God breathed life into man and he became a living soul, we were created to crave eternal connection, a kiss that is never broken. On earth we experience a foretaste of that with our earthly mates. This is a foreshadowing of when we will be joined with Christ as His bride forever and ever, amen. Small wonder the enemy wants to sully this very special gift God has given us to solidify entering into covenant on earth.

Faith

Faith is definitely an act of worship. Jesus wept over people's lack of faith. It angered God when the children of Israel didn't trust Him—didn't have faith in Him. Without faith we can't please God. Small wonder the enemy likes to plant seeds of distrust in our hearts. What pleases God most is loving obedience, which can only come to pass when we have faith. Often the reasons we don't please God are based on our fear that He won't meet us on the other side of our obedience.

What do I mean by that? If I have a sack of seeds, and I see someone who wants to plant a garden, if I don't believe I can get more seeds, I won't be very happy about sharing what I have. If we don't believe God can and will and wants to meet our needs, we'll have great difficulty in following Him, sharing His truths with people, and giving away what He's freely given us because we don't know if more will be coming. Faith is saying we trust God to love us and provide for us.

Humans can be fickle creatures. We won't fight to honor God and defend ourselves and those we know if we don't believe God will be with us and fight for us. We won't follow and obey God if we don't believe He will keep His promises. Instead we'll try to become our own gods and attempt to arrange life to suit us. The very first thing Satan did in the garden was get Eve to question God and His intentions toward her. And he's been using that same strategy to deceive and lead us astray ever since. (You'd think we'd be bored by this strategy by now and not fall for it, but we seem to get sucked in by this trick a lot! We need to make the decision to believe God no matter what.)

Lack of faith is *the* top precursor to sin. What is sin, really? In practical terms it's disobedience to the Word of God. We must remember that the things God says to us are for our good—to protect us and empower us to have the best life. Sin is also any action, thought, word, or state of heart that hurts us or others. This offends and grieves God. It shows a lack of respect for God's creation. It disrupts kingdom living. It creates brokenness, which affects our ability to be holy. God wants us to be holy as in "whole," even as He is holy and whole.

As we trust in Him, we are able to depend on Him to be our sufficiency in all areas of our lives and remain yielded to His Word and His way of walking out our lives. This is worship at its best. This lifestyle that pleases God is counterculture to the world. We obey Him with a spirit of obedience and expectation that He will meet us on the other side of our surrender to Him. Here is where we get to experience kingdom living. As we worship the King of kings, we enter into righteousness, into right standing with Him which leads to peace and, ultimately, the type of joy that can't be taken away because it is a gift given by the Holy Spirit. When we feel the pleasure of God deep in our souls, the Holy Spirit rejoices over our reconciliation. What more can we hope for but to be at peace with our Creator? Truly this is an occasion for worship.

12

Turning the Corner

The woman said to Him, "Sir, I perceive that you are a prophet.
Our fathers worshiped in this mountain, but you people say that
in Jerusalem is the place where men ought to worship."

❧

She allowed his words about all her husbands to penetrate her heart. It was true. There was no denying what he'd said. There it was. The stark reality of her life and the decisions she had made stared her straight in the face. But there was no condemnation from him. He was just stating the facts. No judgments. Just the simple truth. There was no way around it. Nothing to deny. Obviously God had revealed these things to him. How could one contest that? She didn't feel attacked; he had not accused her. As a matter-of-fact, he had been kind in citing her bravery to speak the truth even as veiled as it had been. Nothing in his demeanor had changed toward her. She relaxed now that the truth was out in the open.

She pondered his words. It wasn't just memories that were surfacing. A greater issue was slowly coming to the foreground as she thought about her life overall. What was missing? She could no longer blame her emptiness on a man. There was something deeper going on. Something greater to be realized that went beyond warm arms on a cold night or the certainty of being provided for. There was more than feeling validated in society because you had a partner, legitimate or not. There had to be more. Her thirst returned.

She frowned slightly as she searched through her understanding. Was there something she'd missed? Had she been in search of the wrong thing for her affirmation? Admittedly she did base a large part of her identity on her ability to have a man in her life. Didn't everyone? She didn't like the look of pity that widows and those who had never married received. She'd rather have the disdain for having too many men. But was she wrong in her perspective?

Why did this stranger keep alluding to something that lasted? Something that sounded supernatural? Was there something greater than this natural life that harbored the secret to true fulfillment and peace?

If ever there was a moment to find out, it is now, she decided. After all, this man was a rabbi. If he couldn't answer her questions about God, who could? Sure, she knew what she'd been taught all her life about God, but it seemed so surface right now. So cold and impersonal. God was there, and she was here. If she wanted to reach Him she had to go to where He was. And when she did, she still didn't sense His presence, didn't feel His notice of her or any concern for her estate. What was the point of worshiping someone who didn't respond? Yet her forefathers had worshiped on this mountain. If it was good enough for them, why wasn't it good enough for her?

She licked her lips. She felt so thirsty. The moment she thought of God, the desert within her soul seemed to expand, increasing her desire for water. She thought of an oasis, with sunlight bouncing off the top of the water, playing tricks on the surface by creating twinkles that caught her eye. So if it wasn't a man or financial security or the acceptance of others that could satisfy her, what could? God? Was it possible to have an experience with Him that would set her yearning to rest? Hope leaped inside her spirit.

She inched closer to the stranger, this compassionate teacher. What secrets did he know? He must know something the others didn't. He seemed so serene, and she wanted that serenity too. As hot as it was, there was a coolness that surrounded him. She resisted the urge to reach out and touch him to see if he was as cool as he looked. He had to know something beyond what she'd been taught. She sensed he was her hope for finding what she was searching for. She would take a chance on trusting him…just this once.

There is a day when each one of us comes to the end of ourselves and all the striving ceases. When all the plots and plans for propping up our lives and making things work despite the emptiness inside comes to a halt. We run into a wall of truth: *This is not working. And it hasn't worked for a long time.* Yes, we must come to this point before we are open to taking another look at what we've been searching for. When we finally conclude that all our attempts have failed, we decide we must try something new. An old adage is that "insanity is the practice of doing the same thing over and over again while expecting different results." At some point we have to pull ourselves up short and say, "Wait a minute! What am I doing?" Or, as TV personality Dr. Phil would say, "How is that working for you?"

If it's not working, it's time to do something different. If you're not getting the answers you need, perhaps it's time to ask different questions? The fruit of our choices and the root of our need are two different things. To get the peace and renewal we so deeply crave, we must be willing to dig to the root of our issues. We must decide what we truly value.

I remind people all the time that we can't buy peace. There is no price that will secure it for us. Peace is found between the balance of what we are willing to release and what we are willing to embrace. Are you willing to embrace truth? That is the doorway that leads to the path of peace. You say yes to God's will for your life and joyfully follow His instructions. Are you willing to lay aside the weights and sin of life that so easily hinders you, trips you up, and delays your progress so you can be free to pursue peace? Yes, peace must be pursued. That means decisions have to be made that ensure peace. Weights are different from sins. Weights can be wrong attitudes, wrong thinking, wrong friends, choices, or perspectives. It can be as simple as where you place your trust and what you value. Image versus reality. God versus man. Worship versus taking your life into your own hands and stepping out on the dangerous road of independence.

Eventually all roads of life lead back to God. Are we connected to the right Person to get what we want out of life? Networking is huge today because people realize that worldly success is all about who they know. So who do you know? Who are you connected to? That is the beginning of finding out which doors will open for you and which doors will be shut. Of finding out if you'll gain the type of favor that delivers what you want at no great expense or whether you will pay the ultimate price.

As you find yourself standing before God with empty hands and a scarred heart, the question becomes what or who have you been worshiping. This may reveal the source of your sufferings and your struggles. Where have you been looking for what you've been looking for? What mountain have you climbed only to find nothing at the top? God is waiting...waiting for you to come to the end of yourself, the end of all your attempts and all the things that others have suggested or offered. He is waiting for you to press past religion and come into relationship with Him. Come into the only arms that will hold you forever and guarantee security, peace, fulfillment, and refreshment.

Reflections

1. *What do you worship/value the most?*

2. *In what ways does that satisfy you?*

3. *Does anything seem to be missing in your life right now?*

4. *What do you want out of life? Out of your relationships?*

5. *What are the roots of your areas of disappointment?*

Refreshing Springs

You will become what you worship, so pick your idols carefully. Broken gods only lead to broken places. They have nothing of real value to offer. The Word of God says that at the right hand of Jesus are pleasures ever more—an endless supply of all that we crave, of all that we long for. He says He is the rewarder of those who diligently seek Him, not a man, woman, achievements, or things. Him. It is as simple as that. The more you seek fulfillment in temporal things, the more peace will elude you. The more it eludes you, the more you obsess, sometimes crossing over the line into empty worship. Ah, but there is one Person waiting with open arms who is everything He promised and everything you seek! When you make Jesus Christ your pursuit, your obsession, your worship, you are liberated to receive all you long for. He comes bearing gifts—delightful gifts that promise to fulfill and satisfy. There are great rewards for those who end their fruitless pursuits and, instead, choose to seek God.

13

Seeing the Light

[Jesus said,] "You worship guessing in the dark…
But the time is coming—it has, in fact, come—
when what you're called will not matter and
where you go to worship will not matter.
It's who you are and the way you live
that count before God. Your worship must engage
your spirit in the pursuit of truth. That's the kind of
people the Father is out looking for. Those who are simply
and honestly themselves before him in their worship."

JOHN 4:22-23 MSG

Although there was something liberating about his words, she was almost afraid to believe him. What he said sounded so good. So simple. But it went against the grain of everything she had ever learned. How then did a person prove he or she was good enough to get God's attention? This is where she had been stuck—in the prison of not being good enough, and others had confirmed her train of thought. She'd been there so long now that even if it looked like the door was ajar she was afraid to break her chains and walk away. And yet she longed to do just that.

She wavered. Could the religious leaders in her town be wrong? And what about all the religious teachings she'd been under all her life. Were they wrong? Had they based their entire lives on teachings that weren't accurate? And how could just being herself be good enough before almighty God? Wasn't some sort of posture expected? Some type of ritual demanded? But that was the scary part, what posture or ritual or sacrifice could ever be enough?

And what did he mean by "your worship must engage your spirit in the pursuit of truth"? What would that look like? She'd always done the best she could. She took her offerings and presented them hoping they were enough to cover her sin, to make appeasement for anything that could have offended Him, but how could she know if that really worked? It's all that she knew. All that she had been told. Now here he was saying, "those who worshipped God had to do it out of their very being, their spirits, their true selves, in adoration." This was new to her. It sounded way too simple. She found a safety in the complication of ritual but had to admit there was no core peace or fulfillment. She always walked away wondering if it was enough. There was something empty about it that she couldn't put her finger on.

Was this rabbi suggesting a different way to worship? Was it true that it might not matter whether she was a Jew or a Samaritan? Whether she was a man or a woman? Was this man suggesting she could approach God herself…without the priests interceding for her? That worship might not involve ritual? She wasn't sure if she knew what he meant. Did he believe that every area of her life was potential worship to God? The choices she made, the words she spoke, the things she did?

Something deep inside felt hopeful but hesitant to embrace this new concept. Perhaps ritual was actually easier. It didn't require that anything change in your life, really. You did what you did, made atonement for it, and hoped for the best. There was no joy or release in this process. She wanted something more. Every time she thought of it, her thirst returned. Longing burned her throat with a new urgency. *You are so close, so close!* It was like her very being knew there was truth in what he said, but it was so hard to let go of the rites that had become second nature. Habit. A safe but fruitless exercise. Suddenly she felt exhausted. Exhausted by the rules and regulations. By the human expectations that were never met. By the sameness of everything.

He was right. Her spirit was not engaged. She felt no connection to the One whose rules she followed. Her head and her spirit were at war, one taking a deep breath of relief, the other holding on tremulously to all it knew, afraid of letting go because of the unknown. The type of worship this man spoke of was new, intriguing, refreshing. There was something freeing about the idea of being authentic before God. Being transparent and living out her worship for a God who would respond personally as she paid homage to Him through her everyday actions.

To be able to adore God, to know Him, feel Him, and connect with Him personally. And perhaps it would be easier to obey Him if she felt closer to Him. That thought was like a slap. *This is what has been missing!* Her heart was pounding as she took deep breaths. Why hadn't she heard this idea before?

Then the reminders came. Don't trust this man. When Messiah comes, He will make all things clear. He will make the struggling disappear. *What if this man leads me astray and I miss the Messiah? But how much more wanting could I be?* she thought. The wind howled. She leaned into it, wondering what it would be like to lean into God like that and to feel His sovereign embrace. She could almost imagine it.

***

I was raised Episcopalian. Going to church was purely ritual to us. We went every Sunday morning faithfully. A parishioner who enjoyed listening to my mom and me got us drafted into the choir. We donned our robes with pride, making our way down the center aisle singing songs that sounded grand and important. During the short sermon I would doodle on the church program. After church we would go home and life would go on as usual. The only Sunday I got excited about going to church was Easter because I knew I would get a new outfit.

I also attended Catholic school. We had chapel in the morning before school. I was so fascinated by the priests and the nuns because they looked so regal in their robes while they stroked their rosaries in reverence. I felt they had something I didn't. They seemed so serene. When they bowed their heads to pray, I wanted to lean in and overhear what they were saying. I wondered if they had an "in" with God because of those beads. The nuns seemed to glide across the floor of the chapel, genuflecting so gracefully. I wanted to be one. I used to sneak into the chapel after everyone left and just sit, waiting to see if God would say something and if I would be able to hear Him.

I wanted what the nuns had. They seemed so serene and complete. I thought about it a lot, but I didn't quite know how to ask about what I was feeling. I had this sense of awe whenever I entered that little beautiful chapel with the stained-glass windows and the stations of the cross on the walls. God was there, and I wanted to see Him and know Him. But I didn't know how to connect with Him they way the nuns seemed to be doing. They had given their entire lives to God. Something about that seemed scary but also very beautiful. I didn't realize that even then God was calling me, drawing me to Him.

Shortly after that time we moved to another neighborhood, and I didn't return to Catholic school until high school. By then my fascination and awe of God had diminished. I was distracted by boys and trying to be cool while navigating the waters of being transformed into a young adult. Life went on, and my goal of being a nun was forgotten. In fact, my attitude had changed markedly. I now wondered how anyone could live the way the nuns did. Especially with all the handsome brothers and priests around. I had quite a healthy crush on one brother in particular, whom I decided was way too cute to be taking a vow of celibacy. (The year after I graduated he quit the brotherhood and got married, which confirmed my earlier belief.)

But years later my thirst for God returned. My boyfriend was murdered, and I was devastated. Nothing and no one could comfort me as I descended into the deepest pit of despair imaginable. I thought I would never recover. Then, in the middle of the night, as I perused *The Late Great Planet Earth* by Hal Lindsey, I read the invitation to accept Christ. I put down the book and my Bible and asked Jesus to be my Lord and Savior. It was the first time I felt peace in a long time.

I quickly got involved with a church community and was mentored in the faith. I began to hear the voice of God, and I excitedly went back to my old church to share the news with my pastor. He looked at me as if I'd grown two heads! Suddenly it dawned on me why I had been bored and doodling all those years. It was a beautiful religious place, but the connection with God was being phoned in Sunday after Sunday. I left church dry and wanting every Sunday.

But now I didn't have to depend on church. I had my own line straight to the throne room. I could run into the arms of my loving Abba (Father) when I was broken and disappointed, and He would give me rest. Yes, I could feel the difference. I felt renewed, revived, restored. I found joy in every worship song. I clung to every word of the sermons. I was drinking fresh-squeezed lemonade on a scorching, hot day. Nothing had changed outwardly about my life, but everything had changed inside my heart.

For so long I had battled suicidal thoughts and even unjustly blamed myself for the death of my boyfriend. I felt worthless, like I couldn't get life right. But now God reassured me I was forgiven and made whole in Him. I learned to reach for Him out of my heart instead of my head. With enthusiastic expectation of hearing from Him versus just exercising religious ritual, there was a new joy, a new sense of purpose in my life. I was transformed from a broken woman into a worshiper of the most high God.

The same invitation awaits you—and anyone else—who has come to the end of herself and her search for peace and happiness. Shifting our focus to the root of what we crave—a personal relationship with our Creator—will produce more fruit than all the avenues of seeking to please and fulfill ourselves.

There is something special about drawing close to the One who longs to hold us, love us, and bless us. What may seem like an odd, but good example of this is my dogs. I have three. I love them all, but the one that seeks me out the most touches my heart in a special way. The one who has made me feel like I am his sun, moon, stars, and everything in between is my favorite. He makes me feel loved, and he is deeply loved in return. I have a hard time saying no to anything he wants. Although I want to spoil him, I don't. And I believe God is the same way. All He wants is us—our love, our worship, our adoration, which is manifested in complete surrender and obedience to Him. When He becomes our central focus, the thing we want and seek the most...when giving Him pleasure becomes our chief desire, He meets us and pours His love on us—His rich, healing, cleansing love.

Reflections

1. What or who do you worship?

2. How is your worship manifested?

3. How can your worship be misplaced in your pursuit of fulfillment?

4. In what ways can misplaced worship rob you of the very thing you seek?

5. *How does worshiping the one true God keep your desires in the right perspective?*

Refreshing Springs

Worship is not just for God; it is for you too. In the light of seeing God as He is and celebrating His presence and His power, you gain clarity that puts the affairs of your life into perspective. As you magnify God, He becomes greater than the things you wrestle with. Your struggles are diminished when you remember that He is God and your circumstances are not. They shall not have dominion over you as you lift your hands and worship almighty God, restoring order to your heart and world. As you abide in the shadow of His love, you'll find cooling relief and rest from your struggles. Disappointments become vapors in the light of His comfort. You will be dry and weary no more. You will be at peace. God is your glory and the lifter of your head.

14

Meeting the Messiah

The woman said, "I don't know about that.
I do know that the Messiah is coming. When he arrives,
we'll get the whole story."
"I am he," said Jesus. "You don't have to wait
any longer or look any further."

JOHN 4:25 MSG

S he didn't mean to insult him by not agreeing right away. She just wanted to make sure she was doing the right thing. She wanted so badly to believe what he said, but his words were strange and revolutionary. They suggested so much freedom for someone used to rules and rigidity. She wasn't sure what he was talking about. But she *did* know there was a promised Messiah who would return and liberate them. Everyone spoke of Him—this conquering warrior who would deliver them from the oppression they suffered under. Yes, when He came everything would be put right. Perhaps in that day she would finally have peace. Her heart wouldn't ache, and life wouldn't be so hard. Matters would be settled once and for all. She didn't know exactly how He would fix everything, she just knew He would. This Messiah everyone longed for would set them free from evil and unrighteousness. No one seemed to know when He was coming, only that He was. All the blanks would be filled in then because He would know all things and possess all power.

She sighed. She prayed this was true, and that He would come soon. *How miserable to hope and wish and pray for something that would never be a reality,* she thought. *Life would be in vain.* All the standards they held and lived for would be for naught. A shiver ran down her spine even though it was the hottest time of day. *What does a person live for if he or she doesn't have a promise of something better? Of someone to place hope in? Someone greater than us?* The thought of there not being Someone who possessed greater power over her circumstances than she did filled her with horror. A life without God was terrifying. Though she wasn't the most obedient or law-keeping person, she found comfort in knowing she could offer penance to God.

And what of hope? If in this earthly life alone she had hope and nothing greater awaited, she would be most miserable of women. There had to be something better than this. There had to be a promise of a different world, a different life—a place where struggling ceased and she could find rest. There had to be redemption from all that threatened to devour her soul. Was this just the desperate cry of her heart or was the Messiah and God and heaven a reality? She chose to believe they were real. Even as she asked for clarity, she hoped the stranger would have an answer. And he did…but it wasn't the answer she expected. He said He was the Messiah!

As she considered His words, she realized she'd never considered what the Messiah would look like or how He would appear. Deep in her soul she knew His words were true. She'd known He was different from the first moment He'd spoken to her. *He is the Messiah! That explains everything—His kindness, His compassion, His lack of judgment.*

What did this mean for her? What was she to do with this amazing revelation?

"You don't have to wait any longer or look any further," He said. That sounded so good. But now that the moment she'd been waiting for was here, what now?

We humans complicate life far more than necessary. We are a conflicted people. We want rules; we hate rules. We seek the safety of boundaries; we resent being limited or reined in. We exhaust ourselves trying to figure everything out and then land in an exhausted heap crying for somebody to save us—from our circumstances, from ourselves, from other people. "Just save us, Lord!" And yet when we consider the simplicity of His grace, it seems too good to be true. Pride tells us we should actively *atone* and then *earn* our redemption, while humility tells us we should simply be grateful for His love and grace and salvation.

The tension of accepting that we will never be good enough in our own efforts to fulfill God's standards fights our flesh that is urging us to try. This is religion at it's best—or should I say worst? "Religion" wants to take the credit for goodness, while "relationship" simply means we want to enjoy God's embrace. Having a personal relationship with our Father in heaven means we can bask in the fullness of His love and allow it to transform our hearts and minds. Change us from the inside out. Cause us to walk in holiness because our greatest desire is to please Him because He loves us so much. What incredible joy!

As we submerge ourselves in God's love, there is no struggle to surrender. There is no rending of our rights because we gladly release ourselves to God's desires because He is all we truly want. When we love Him and accept His gift of salvation through Jesus Christ, we are made whole, liberated to walk in holiness and fully experience the rewards of kingdom living: right standing with God, the peace that accompanies that reconciliation, and the joy that comes from being loved as we are.

Isn't this astounding and terrific news! The King of kings and Lord of lords deems us precious and acceptable. We breathe easier knowing we are loved, adopted, and accepted in spite of our flaws. There is liberty in being His children. There is wholeness in confessing our brokenness and allowing Him to mend us. This is how He reveals who He is. By being everything that He promised and so much more. This is where our searching ends.

Reflections

1. *What beliefs have kept you from experiencing the joy of a true, personal relationship with Jesus Christ?*

2. *Where do you struggle with His grace at work in your life?*

3. *What hopes do you harbor relating to the redemptive work of Christ in you?*

4. *When is it most difficult for you to embrace His grace?*

5. *What would convince you even more of God's love for you?*

Refreshing Springs

So many people strive to be worthy of God's blessings, yet there is no price, no act, no exercise that can attain this lofty aspiration. The grace of God is what it is—simply grace. Unmerited, unearned, the gift of God's grace seems too good to be true—but true it is. No waiting in line and no time perimeters. Redemption is instant the moment we accept it from God. Jesus restores your worth and qualifies you for this precious gift that He is so passionate about giving. After all is said and done, all the avenues have been explored, and we have gone hither, thither, and yon, we find Him patiently waiting for us to turn to Him. And when we do, we make a wonderful discovery: He is our great reward! Truly all that we long for is found in Him.

PART 5

What Is True Nourishment?

We have a tendency to cling to what we have, even if it doesn't fully satisfy, especially when we don't know something greater awaits. As long as we are living beneath our godly means, we remain dissatisfied and open to offense because, frankly speaking, others recognize when we are not living the life we ought to be. Only when we face our fears and embrace our true callings will hope spring eternal, urging us on to find lasting fulfillment in Christ. Disappointment can be transformed into powerful life lessons and pain can be translated into power as we finally locate what truly nourishes us, mind, soul, and body.

What we believe we need to make us truly happy rarely does. Locating the true source of nourishment and refreshing is the only way we are able to lay aside the weights and sins that so easily hinder us from moving forward as we follow God. He has a better life in mind for us. One that is rich with heavenly nourishment that gives us strength.

Beyond the real, physical food we eat, we need to understand that we must nourish ourselves spiritually, and that what we put out is just as important as what we are putting in. "Man does not live on bread alone, but on every word that comes from the mouth of God" (Matthew 4:4 NIV). Many of us mistake our spiritual hunger for something else.

Spiritual hunger can often be mistaken for physical hunger. We eat but are not satisfied. We have no idea what we are truly craving, so we keep eating, heightening our frustration and expanding our waistlines. And all the time God is calling, saying to us, "Why do you eat that which does not satisfy? Come and listen to Me! Eat what is good and let your soul delight in fatness (Isaiah 55:2). It's so good to know that we can be fat in the spirit and still look good on the outside. In fact, we will look even better. When we fill our souls with the right things, our bodies will crave less. Remember, whatever you feed the most remains the strongest.

There is a God-sized hole in all of us that nothing but God can fill and satisfy. Seeking to fill it with anything else deepens our cravings for fulfillment, robs us of peace, and frustrates our hopes. Part of effective kingdom living is choosing to fill up on the right things.

Output is just as important as input in any dietary regime. How we burn calories helps determine if we stay lean and mean or if we become sluggish and unmotivated. What keeps us energized and flooded with hope and excitement is exercising what God has placed in us, thereby fulfilling our purpose.

As Jesus shared with the woman at the well in the heat of the day, He was being rejuvenated. Meanwhile the disciples had left to buy food. When they returned they found him talking to this solitary woman. Soon after they arrive she leaves her water jar behind and heads into town, a strange move on her part, yet they didn't linger on her actions. Their focus was Jesus. They were sure He had to be hungry, especially after waiting in the sun so long without food. They were surprised to find that He wasn't hungry at all! Had he eaten something already? Perhaps the strange woman had given him some bread? No? Jesus then makes the strange statement that He has food they know nothing of. What did that mean?

Sitting at the well and talking to the woman, revealing profound spiritual truths, including His being the Messiah, must have been so fulfilling and gratifying for Jesus! He was strengthened and energized by walking in His God-given purpose and changing lives. For every healing, for every transformation that He instigated as He walked the earth, undoubtedly He felt full—full of purpose, full of life, full of destiny, full of joy. This is what He came for and lived for. He was clear on this. "My food is to do the will of him who sent me" (John 4:34). That's it. Bottom line.

When we step into God's purposes for us, touching the people we are supposed to touch, we are filled to the brim with excitement and satisfaction. There is a deep fulfillment from being "in the God zone," the path you know you're supposed to be on. Everything in your spirit sings, "Yes, this is the life!" This doesn't mean we won't encounter challenges and hardships, but even in those we know God's love and care and joy. Whether we are making money or not, we feel full and invigorated. (And this is a good test for motivation. Ask, "If money weren't an issue, what would I do with my life?" The answer will reveal what your passion and purpose really are.) Jesus knew His purpose, walked in it, and was fed spiritually.

When the woman at the well got the revelation of who Jesus was and what true worship was all about, she stepped into God's purpose and her priorities changed instantly. The water she came seeking became the last thing on her mind. She was driven by something more urgent at the core of her soul. She had to tell others what she'd just heard. She turned and left her water jar at the well and headed back into town to share the good news with the people who weren't accepting of her.

Purpose inspired by God looks past offenses to accomplish its mission. Its focus is elsewhere. It concentrates on an eternal picture, looking past the immediate things that get in the way of fulfilling destiny. A purpose-driven individual is able to discern what is truly important so he or she can stay in the correct lane until reaching the destination. God-focused people are aware that every moment is precious and counts for the kingdom. There is no time or room for distractions.

The Samaritan woman heads into town to share her news and encourage people to go see the man she believes is the Messiah. And the people go to the well. There is no mention of stopping for snacks along the way. There is no concession stand by the well. Food was the last thing on anyone's mind that afternoon. They had finally found what they were truly hungry for. As they lingered in the presence of Jesus, they were fed true nourishment. Rich and deeply satisfying. Filling. Their hunger was finally abated. Their faith was strengthened. They found new life and restoration. Their purposes were clarified. There was a reason for living besides going through the motions of the day-to-day. This simple realization added a dynamic dimension to everyday living that changed everything. Now that they were full, there was room for hope.

15

Free to Let Go

*Just then his disciples came back. They marveled that he
was talking with a woman, but no one said,
"What do you seek?" or, "Why are you talking with her?"
So the woman left her water jar and went away into town
and said to the people, "Come, see a man who told me
all that I ever did. Can this be the Christ?"*

John 4:27-29 esv

⸎

The men didn't say it, but the looks on their faces did. She saw the
curiosity in their eyes as they approached the stranger whom she
knew to be the Messiah. His followers weren't like Him, that was for
sure. Judgment was etched on their faces as they took her in. Their eyes
calculated her position in life and her motives for talking to their rabbi.
Oh yes, she knew that look, but for the first time she didn't flinch. Obviously He had trained them well. They didn't question Him, though

their eyes betrayed their curiosity and misgivings. *Of course they wonder why He is speaking with me,* she thought. *After all, I did at first too.* But now she knew this was no ordinary man with an ordinary agenda. He was different. He made her feel different, so different that her usual sensitivities were dissolved. Before her encounter with Messiah, she would have raised her head, tilting her chin upward for effect to put up her guard and keep the men in their place. To silently dare them to approach her. But now their opinion was irrelevant. She'd found what she was looking for, and it wasn't the approval or acceptance of men.

She'd had that and found it wasn't enough. She'd also had their disapproval, and found it to be a deep wound that wouldn't heal—until now. Suddenly what she lived for before no longer mattered. Her entire perspective had changed. A light had come on in her soul that illuminated her understanding. She wasn't the sum total of what others thought. She was who she'd always been—a woman valued by God. What was in her wasn't rearranged by the opinions of others. Her power as a God-created woman wasn't diminished unless she failed to use it. Her value wasn't decreased unless she chose to cheapen herself.

She was valued; a force to be reckoned with in her own right. What she possessed inwardly couldn't be taken away unless she chose to give it away. No, she no longer cared what they thought. Her Messiah loved her. He hadn't pulled back. Nothing about His demeanor had changed. He showed no shame for having an exchange with her. Nothing about His countenance suggested He was embarrassed or sorrowed for talking with her. His gaze hadn't broken. He was waiting to see the impact of His words on her heart. She knew this instinctively. It was one thing to say she believed what He'd said, but how would that be revealed through her life? How would His revelation play out in her actions?

Suddenly she felt an urgency to tell others. *Will they believe me?* It was a fleeting thought in the face of her passion. She couldn't possibly keep this good news to herself. She set the water jar down. Water was not her primary focus right now. The thirst of the others she knew was. It seemed useless to struggle back toward town with the jar, full or empty. She had something more important to share. Physical thirst had been a mere distraction from her true thirst. And now that she knew this, she wanted others to meet the Messiah too. She had seen the empty looks in their eyes. Their disapproval of her only veiled it temporarily. She had used it to justify in her mind that she was just as good as they were, that they weren't better than she was and their lives weren't more important. *We all choose our own flavor of poison,* she'd said to herself.

Now she knew just what they needed. She would find a way to get them to come and meet the Messiah. If she was wrong they would know it. But what if she was right? It didn't seem fair to keep such good news to herself. Though these people had hurt her, the joy she felt right now erased it. She felt no evidence of the sting that had pierced her soul at their put-downs before. She was free. Unhindered. Whole. And she knew this could not be taken from her…ever.

She turned her back on the men talking with the Messiah and turned toward town to find the ones she knew harbored their own unanswered queries. With each step she took she felt an urgent sense of purpose rising inside her. She disciplined herself not to run in the overpowering heat. She would get there soon enough, and her news would be the same. She had met the Messiah! The one everyone was waiting for! She was the most unlikely person to be the bearer of such wonderful tidings. *How is that for God's sense of humor?* she thought with a laugh. Again a shadow rolled through her mind as if cast by a rolling thistle: *Will the people receive this news from me?* She shrugged. *That's their choice.* She would say what she knew and leave the rest to them—and to the Messiah.

Her timing was perfect. The town had begun to stir as people began to fill the streets, returning from their retreat from the sun. A familiar face looked her way, and she moved toward him and the men he was talking to. She could see the reserve in his eyes, as if he were steeling himself against whatever she wanted of him in broad daylight. But she wasn't put off. She wanted nothing from him! She'd already found what she needed.

As soon as she was near, she spilled out her experience like a river dashing over stones. *"Come, see a man who told me all that I ever did! Can this be the Christ?"* Her voice rose, capturing the attention of others as her words tumbled over themselves. A crowd gathered. The reserve was gone, replaced by curiosity and, yes, thirst and excitement. Their eyes followed her finger pointing in the direction of Jacob's well. The crowd moved forward, heading toward the well, their questions flying.

"Where did the stranger come from?"

"How did he know about her?"

"What did he say exactly?"

"Is this man a prophet from God?"

Let's just go and meet him ourselves.

She followed behind, struggling to keep up. They would see soon enough that she was right. She knew it in her heart and soul. Her heart leaped with joy every time she remembered her conversation with the Messiah. She wondered if He would look into their eyes and tell them about themselves too. What would He reveal? Would He tell them straight out that He was the Messiah like He did for her?

Yes, He was still there. Calmly sitting by the well surrounded by his companions, who looked a bit more wary than He did. She quivered when she saw Him as hope filled her. She couldn't wait to hear Him speak again. She thirsted for more of Him. Her eyes caught sight of the jar she'd left behind. It was dwarfed by her view of him. *How strange,* she thought. *I practically ran into town and back, and yet I don't feel thirsty or tired.*

How is it that we can want something so badly that we think we can't live without it? That is, we feel that way until something "better" comes along. You and I spend so much time trying to fill the empty spaces in our hearts and souls. We jump to inconclusive conclusions of what will fulfill us. We cling to these things even when it becomes clear they aren't going to do the trick. We hold on for dear life, bound by the uncertainty of what awaits if we let go. And though we know that something is not necessarily better than nothing, the threat of nothing is very real. Fear keeps us glued to temporary moments of gratification and fleeting moments of fulfillment even as the yawning chasms in our souls increase.

What would happen if we let go of that horrible job we hate? If we told that man who drains the life from us goodbye? What would happen if we trusted God with our children, no matter how wayward they got? What would happen if we moved? What would happen if we simply let go of the thing we keep praying to be delivered from? Liberty is just a reflex away. Healing is just a breath away…exhale. Breathe. Let go.

I recall the story of a man who fell off a cliff one night. On the way down he managed to grab hold of a branch. He clung to it desperately, waiting for light and help to come. As he hung there praying, he heard the words, "Let go." He thought he was hearing things, and he clung tighter. Again the voice came. "Let go." He clung even tighter. Shortly after the sun rose, the man looked down fearfully to see how far he would fall should he grow too tired to hold on any longer. The ground was waiting to welcome him a mere foot below where he was hanging.

So often this is our lot in life. Deliverance is just around the bend if we will only trust God enough to let go and depend on Him. God says He knows the plans He has for us (Jeremiah 29:11). The problem is that we don't know what He has up His divine sleeve, so we have to trust. This is where we all get into trouble. Our fears affect our obedience. Without faith it is impossible to obey and please God. If we don't believe He will keep His promises and meet us on "the other side of our obedience," we are prone to take our lives into our own hands and hang on for dear life. When our hands are wrapped around something, it's hard to reach out and grab or receive anything else. This is the tension between control and release. Perhaps this is why God patiently waits for us to get to the end of ourselves, to get to where we are so weary we surrender. I long to get to this place willingly, but so often my human will and fear get in the way. I am always embarrassed to find that a greater blessing awaited me even as I stubbornly held on to what I already had. But as I reluctantly open my hands and experience God's greater blessing, I think, *How could I have second-guessed God? When will I finally reach the place where I stand open and expectant instead of clinging and doubtful?*

And this is when He reveals Himself. In the midst of my trembling and questioning, He turns on the light and pours me rivers of refreshment that strengthen me for the journey when I finally let go. Finally I discover that what I was clinging to was mere dust, and not so important or life-changing after all. What I thought I needed turned out to be a mere want, even a passing fancy in light of discovering what I truly needed all along—God. God and the revelation of what He has planned for me.

I open my hands and realize letting go isn't all that difficult after all. There is great reward in it because I finally get to embrace what God has for me, and it is healing, liberating, and fulfilling. I find myself like the woman at the well—able to face what I was running from because I am now rooted in God. I am no longer dependent on external factors to fulfill internal needs. I am satisfied. I want no more. I am strong enough to walk in the light of Jesus Christ and show others the way to Him. No longer hindered by past mistakes and choices, I face the future ready to grasp new beginnings and dismiss old claims against me. With the revelation of who Christ is comes the revelation of who I am. And my identity in Him is unshakeable and unchangeable. The opinions of others don't change who God said I am. My value can't be decreased nor is my power to overcome all things in Him diminished. I am free to fling open my arms and let go...let go and embrace all God has for me.

Reflections

1. What do you cling to for security?

2. What is your greatest fear?

3. What do you believe will happen if you let go of that fear?

4. What would it take for you to let go?

5. What does your heart long for most? How does not letting go hinder you from receiving this?

Refreshing Springs

God's plan for you includes wholeness, hope, and a future. Because He is leading you, you have nothing to fear. He loves you. Only in God's kingdom does complete surrender get you more than you could gain by continuing to fight to get what you want. Oh how God desires to set you free from yourself and bind you to His heart and His promises where fullness of life awaits. He will complete you and satisfy your longings. Nothing will want in your life because in Him you live and breathe and have your very being. In Him you have all things pertaining to life and godliness. There is no longer a tendency to hunger or thirst, for He is your sufficiency. Finally you can let go.

16

Released to Hope

Many Samaritans from that town believed in him because
of the woman's testimony, "He told me all that
I ever did." So when the Samaritans came to him,
they asked him to stay with them, and he stayed there
two days. And many more believed because of his word.

JOHN 4:39-41 ESV

S he felt different. She must have looked different too. She knew
others had noticed the difference. That they were struck by it. The
fact they'd been willing to listen and follow her request spoke volumes.
Even they recognized hope when they saw it. Yes, that was the word.
She had hope! She radiated hope. And she wanted others to have it too.
No offense was large enough to cloud her vision of the endless possibilities before her. She threw her head back and laughed. The fresh air felt
good. It was as if she were breathing for the very first time.

The people kept questioning her along the way. "What did he say?" "How did he know everything about you?" On and on the questions went. She tried to answer them as best she could by repeating her conversation with the stranger. They stopped short when she told them how He knew about all of her husbands and her present situation. She could hear audible gasps as the crowd slowed their steps. She didn't know if their shock was due to her honesty or if they were pondering whether they wanted to be in a position of exposure like that. What if He uncovered their secrets in front of everyone?

But then she told them of His kindness. His lack of judgmental attitude. Their shoulders relaxed, and their strides quickened again. The air crackled with curiosity and excitement. What would the stranger tell them? As they approached, she stepped forward, drawing closer to Him, beckoning to the others to come 'round. They were all suddenly quiet, ready to hear what this Jew had to say. She turned to Him, and her expression said it all. Her face shone with faith; her eyes were alight with expectation. She nodded, silently saying, "Go ahead, tell them! Tell them what you told me."

Yes, she could only tell her own version but in order for them to truly believe they had to have their own encounter with Him. Though what He spoke was universal truth, each person gathered there would personalize His words and apply them to their own circumstances. Their individual fears, hopes and concerns would sift His words through their own hearts and hear them differently according to their need.

In His words she had heard more than a redemption story. She had heard hope for true love that would last forever, peace, and security beyond her wildest dreams. She'd heard that she wasn't alone. She didn't know the needs of the other villagers, but she knew the Messiah would. It was a mystery how He knew people inside and out, but after a while it didn't matter. There was such healing in being known and accepted in spite of yourself. The people welcomed the Messiah; and the Messiah welcomed them. The suspense was over. They were accepted. There was redemption and hope.

There have been moments in my life where I lost hope. Those moments are the darkest nights of my soul. I recall the hopelessness that surrounded me after the death of a boyfriend. We had argued. He had traveled, walking away angry. We both thought time would cool our tempers and heal the issue, but we were robbed of that moment. He was killed while on vacation, and I couldn't snatch the moment back… the hurtful words, the misunderstanding. In a heated moment, his best friend said it was my fault this man I truly loved had been in the wrong place at the wrong time and taken a bullet. The words pierced my heart and settled in to stay. In those cold and lonely nights I rehashed those words. And every time I did, I moved further away from hope and closer to despair.

It was my fault. The words rang in my head at the most inopportune moments, reducing me to tears. I sought relief from the pain in the wrong ways. Anything that I thought would soothe the nerves left too raw and open. No amount of mood-altering substances silenced the words in my head. In fact, they intensified the pain and magnified the internal accusations: *It's all your fault. You are worthless. Beyond hope. Undeserving of love. Look at the mess that you've made. Who would want you? Your relationships never work out.* The assaults rained on, drenching me with overwhelming loss. There was no hope.

Until one day I met a woman on a bus who invited me to church. After several weeks of avoidance, I finally went with her. I was harboring a tsunami of tears thinly veiled beneath the surface of my soul. As the service wore on, I wanted to release the flood but held my peace. I prayed the end of the service was near so I could escape back to my corner of the world where no one would witness my excruciating pain. But no, the preacher was looking at me. He was beckoning me to come forward. I didn't want to. I was sure I wouldn't survive the walk to the front without exploding. I couldn't bear it. But all eyes were on me, and there was nowhere to run, no place to hide.

I rose from my chair and made the endless journey to the altar. It seemed like years passed by as I slowly made my way to the front. I was completely unprepared for what happened next. This tender man of God laid his hands on my head and began to tell me how much God loved me and that He had a plan for my life. God knew my pain and wanted me to know that I was loved. That I was forgiven. Could I forgive myself? The dam broke. How did the preacher know what I needed? But then again, I didn't care. The only thing I cared about was that God loved me. In spite of my foolishness and bad choices, He loved me. There was hope for my life. Walking back to my seat, I was a new woman. Something had been given to me that could not be taken away. God loved me! He had gone out of His way to meet me where I was. He used a stranger to tell me the Good News! All was not lost. I was forgiven, loved, saved.

The change in my countenance was marked. People at work noticed immediately. It was drastic. This chain-smoking, loud talking, party animal was transformed. It was such a flip of the script that people asked me outright, "What happened to you?" And I told them. I told them I met a Man who told me everything I'd ever done. I invited them to church, and they came. They not only came, they met the same Man and found their own redemption! I had my own section of church with all the harvest God granted to me. I was a voice crying in the wilderness, "Repent!" I was beckoning in the desert of corporate America, "Come and see!" I wouldn't take no for an answer and rarely had to because I was a changed woman, the evidence of God's power was palpable in my life. I was different. I looked different. I carried myself differently. I approached life differently. My choices were different. None of this was missed by those around me. I was changed! All because I had a Savior and hope. And people wanted hope too, so they came. Their newfound hope in Christ gave others hope and the message expanded beyond my limited sphere of influence.

My faith was contagious. Creating a thirst in the people I met. The more I shared my faith, the more I became entrenched in it. I felt more alive than ever. No magic wand had been waved to make everything all right. The man I loved was still gone. I still had the same struggles in other areas of my life. But now I dealt with them in a new way because I had hope in Christ, and that hope freed me.

Reflections

1. What situation seems unsalvageable in your life?

2. What would it take to restore your hope?

3. What types of things have been setbacks that make it difficult for you to embrace hope?

4. In what ways would a support system help to encourage your faith?

5. In what ways can a testimony be a powerful way of building your faith and restoring hope?

Refreshing Springs

Hope is powerful. Its appearance draws people to the ones exhibiting it. People know it when they see it, though they might not be able to put their finger on exactly what it is about you that is telling them to press in. They want what you have. Share your hope in Christ with them! The more you do, the more it increases in your life. For this very reason, dare to move past your pain, realizing that without pain hope wouldn't be as attractive. In the moments of restoration we most appreciate the touch of God and hang on His every word. Those who are forgiven much, love much and find solace in the arms of the One who knows everything about them and loves them anyway. His tender mercies are new every morning, and shine especially bright after a dark night of the soul.

17

Fulfilling Destiny

*They said to the woman, "It is no longer because of
what you said that we believe, for we have
heard for ourselves, and we know that this is indeed
the Savior of the world."*

S he couldn't claim credit for their transformation. And, indeed, they
had all been changed by their time spent with this stranger…no—
He was their Messiah. She had been a conduit, a catalyst for their journey toward hope and redemption. *Who would have guessed,* she thought,
*that one who had caused tongues to wag in the worst way would end up
spearheading a revival? Who could have imagined that the same ones who
shunned and despised her would follow her, believe her, and embrace what
she had embraced. Unbelievable!* But it was true. The Messiah made all

the difference. He had changed her, and that change began a domino effect that set an entire town abuzz with excitement and newness of life.

As the people escorted Jesus into town, urging him to stay and talk with them, the woman followed a few steps behind, lost in her thoughts. How quickly a life can change. When she woke up this morning she hadn't anticipated anything remarkable happening. It was a day like any other day. The same old routine awaited her. She had prayed no special prayer that morning. She had done the usual things she'd always done before setting off for the well. She remembered sighing as she looked toward the well and considered the trek. She wondered how much longer life could go on this way. She hoped and wished for a breakthrough that would birth something different in her world, but she never expected anything new to happen. Her life stretched out before her as endlessly as the road that led away from Samaria to parts unknown. Though she'd wondered what was beyond her limited view, she had no expectancy or drive or hope of knowing.

And now she marveled at how one conversation changed everything. Had she been born for this moment? Could it be that all the heartbreak and disappointment she had experienced was culminated in this one event? Was her suffering the tool that was needed to draw others? Was brokenness the path to grace?

She thought of a time when she was much surer of herself. It was before the winds of life and change assaulted her heart and wounded her. She wouldn't have given the stranger at the well the time of day. She'd been in control of her world. She was full. The only thirst she had was for more of what she already indulged in. And then it happened. *Loss* came suddenly, swiftly knocking her off balance, cracking her perfect veneer. She watched the contents of her life spilling out before her. She managed to plug the hole, but it widened in the years to come as setback after setback and disappointment after disappointment took its toll. The beautiful vessel she once was lost its smooth finish. No longer luminous and now porous, she was dry and empty. She became a survivor, settling for momentary glimpses of refreshing.

But now she would never be empty again. Her joy bubbled up,

reminding her of a clear brook chasing quiet ripples over smooth stones in a rush toward the stream that fed it. She was energized, renewed… yes, refreshed! She was heady with the realization that the newness she felt was greater than her and for a purpose beyond her own satisfaction. Her life could make a difference! She was significant. She was part of something greater than herself. She was created for this moment, and everything that had occurred was a setup leading to this moment. This was her destiny.

In the days that followed, and after the Messiah had departed for Galilee, she hummed to herself as she made her way back to the well. She nodded at one of her neighbors who smiled and waved. *Fancy that!* The town had been transformed too. The atmosphere had changed. She had only been the catalyst. On the outside looking in, people might have thought everything was very much the same in the village in terms of function. But some things had been, well, let's just say "set aright." The same rudiments of life, the same schedule, but now there was a new sense of purpose.

The woman who had met Jesus at the well first now went there for a different reason. No longer driven by thirst, it was a place where she recaptured that first encounter and dwelt on the goodness of God. She saw Him in everything now. She had been transformed into a true worshiper. In the light of her new attitude, she found infinite reasons for praise and thanksgiving. And her joy and faith were erasing the scars of her former disappointments. The memories were still there, but they no longer bore deep impressions into her psyche. She no longer walked in fear of the next shoe dropping in her life. No longer did she anticipate more disappointments. Nor was she ruled by despair and emptiness any longer. As she threw open the shutters on the windows of her home, she flung open her heart in anticipation of all things praiseworthy for at last she had hope.

Reflections

1. *What test has God transformed into a testimony of hope in your life?*

2. *What was your initial response to what you were going through?*

3. *What have you learned from your experience?*

4. *In what way has God glorified Himself to you through this experience?*

5. *How can you use your former pain to help others?*

Refreshing Springs

Sometimes you think you don't have the strength to squeeze the lemons life hands you, but make lemonade you must. And not just for yourself, but also for others. There is fellowship in suffering. Brokenness is beautiful when the contents are poured out to reveal what was hidden within. Smooth and beautiful, worn from hard stones it bore so long. Time with God produces wisdom and grace. There is a wearing on your soul that prepares you to step into a destiny that can't be short-circuited or overstepped. God will complete His work in you. And He is determined to perfect all things concerning you. In the end, you will become a vessel of honor for His glory. What you contain is precious—a hope that doesn't make you ashamed. You have endured trials, persevered, and come out on the other side—proof again that your hope in Christ is not in vain.

PART 6

Your Life Today

Transformation is beautiful. It is the most compelling evangelism tool we can use. Consider the words of the townspeople to the Samaritan woman: "We no longer believe just because of what you said; now we have heard for ourselves, and we know that this man really is the Savior of the world" (John 4:39 NIV).

It will always come to this. You can lead a horse to water, but you can't make him drink. He has to be thirsty, first of all. And the water has to be inviting. But most important, it has to taste good when he drinks it. What does your life look like? Is it inviting? Does it compel others to seek what you have? Do people want to follow when you point to a Man named Jesus? Does your conversation and lifestyle leave a good taste in the mouths of others?

What Does Your Life Reflect?

❧

Although it's almost a cliché, it's true that our lives are the only Bible some people will read. We are living testimonies of the love and power of God to the world. I find it interesting that even those who don't profess to be Christians seem to know what Christianity should look like. They know when "Christians" have crossed the line and aren't behaving in a Christlike manner. When that happens, the enemy of our souls is quick to use them to condemn us and attempt to tear down our witness for Christ.

I often try to imagine what Jesus looked like. What His demeanor was like. What His responses and reactions to things were. What about Him caused people to follow Him? There was something special. Perhaps today we would say He had charisma, but I believe there was a peace that surrounded Him that drew others in. He was an enigma. Not easily ruffled by anything anyone did or said. Seldom moved to anger. He felt no need to explain or defend Himself. He was uncompromising. He had a way of making people feel significant. His words healed more people than His hands did. He was confident in who He was and to whom He belonged. He did not demand His rights. He walked His talk. When faced with conflict, He moved past it, leaving others to writhe in their anger. He didn't insist on being accepted. He spoke the truth in love with conviction. He was accessible and sensitive to the needs of others. He was practical—heavenly minded but also down to earth. He looked at people through God's eyes and saw their potential. Everyone was a candidate for redemption. Although He had the power to judge, He didn't (John 8:16; 12:47). His Father would do that. His job was to tell the Good News that the kingdom was at hand.

I think of the profound story of the woman caught in adultery and brought to him (John 8). He was not shocked or rocked by what she had done. He addressed her accusers first. "Let him who is without sin among you be the first to throw a stone at her." He was quietly suggesting they check their hearts on this sin issue before sentencing others. The same measure of grace we give is what we will receive (Matthew 7:2). As they silently slinked away one by one, the woman was left standing in front of Jesus. He looked up and told her to go and not sin again. This struck me deeply the first time I read it because Jesus could have stoned her within the law. *He* was without sin. Yet He did not flaunt His purity and perfection. He sympathized with her humanity without excusing it. He gave her the opportunity to choose the right life.

I asked myself if I emulated Jesus when confronted with the sins of others. Words are one thing but we know actions speak louder. The way we carry ourselves, our countenances, and our responses tell people the true story about who we are. The little flashes of temper, the quick judgments, the rash decisions, the impulsive actions, the acts of being defensive, these things can cause the people around us to question where we stand with Jesus. There is an expectation from the world that people who call themselves Christians live according to a higher law so they will rise above the fray of the world. So they're disappointed when they see us fall short of God's mark…or what they perceive to be God's mark. As we grow in Christ we should become more like Him and less like how we were before we met Him.

Going back to the woman at the well, there was something about her countenance that compelled people to follow her to Jesus. That something is what I hope every believer will possess. We can't force anyone to believe in Christ or to live a holy life, but we most certainly can be positive influences. We can be catalysts that compel them to seek a better, higher way of living.

The Bible says we are the salt that should make people thirsty for God. We are lights that should invite others to come out of the darkness (Matthew 5:13-16). But too many times our message isn't edible because it's over-seasoned with sharp, cutting judgments that don't reflect the heart of God. Too many times our light is harsh, glaring so much that people cover their eyes and prefer the darkness. Though called to "not be in the world," we are not called to repel people from the kingdom either. We are to be like Jesus, walking in peace with God and calling people to God.

We should walk our talk in such a way that people will follow us or approach us, intrigued by what we possess: the love of God and His peace, which passes all understanding. The kind of joy that is not diminished by external circumstances. Faith that triumphs in the face of adversity. Grace and compassion for others. Wisdom from above that gives life. Are you making God an attraction in your life? Ultimately, the core of a purpose-driven life is to live the mandate given to mankind in the garden. To be fruitful and multiply. Multiplication of the kingdom will not occur if we are not fruitful spiritually as well as naturally. Spiritual fruit is the evidence that God is present and at work in our lives. That living for Him is fulfilling, productive, and joyful. When we are intimate with God, we bear the fruit of His Spirit, the attributes of Christ to the world—love, joy, peace, patience, kindness, goodness, faithfulness, gentleness, and self-control (Galatians 5:22). These attributes in us will draw people to Christ.

Resisting the devil and submitting to God so that our lives glorify God by reflecting His traits and values also causes people to look to Christ because they see Him at work in us.

This should be one of the main goals of every believer. Our personal relationship with Christ is the fuel that drives us to share His work of transformation in us. This type of testimony doesn't occur in flashes, but is lived through the consistency of lives that have been truly changed by the living God. This is the evidence that the world finds compelling.

Satan tries so hard to mar the beauty of what God has done for us. Don't let him. Choose to be transparent, vulnerable, and humble in light of who we were when we weren't surrendered to God and model who we are now in Christ. Through Christ, the woman at the well knew her undone state. She was aware of how much she needed redemption. She knew she was a hopeless case but through the Messiah she was made whole. The hope she found in Him she immediately shared with others so they could also experience His life-changing love. We have the power to do the same!

Cool Waters

W hat is your story? Every woman has one. Each story eventually gets to God's story if you keep on walking. He waits at the various wells in our lives, meeting us at every turning point. Scripture doesn't tell us if the woman at the well ever saw Jesus again, but I suspect she did. Why do I say that? Because one encounter with Christ isn't enough. In the course of a lifetime we revisit the well and find ourselves wanting all over again. Such are the seasons of life and the inconsistencies of humanity. We are prone to take our lives back into our own hands time and time again until we mature into complete dependence on Him. In our immaturity we fight for our independence like spoiled babies too tired to stay awake, yet too ready to go to sleep. We struggle to take charge of our lives. But the more spiritually mature we get, the wiser we get. It is profound to note that the more we know the more we realize we don't know at all about ourselves, about life, about God.

I am a terrible gardener, but this much I've learned about keeping my spirit well-hydrated with the Word from the little garden I attempted to have one summer. I bought the troughs and selected a beautiful array of flowers to be planted in them. I was so proud of my little English garden on my balcony until the flowers drooped and looked pitiful. I poured water into the troughs, but it only ran straight out the other end. I was mortified. How was I to keep the water from seeping out of the bottom? I poured in more, and this time less water drained through. I waited about a half hour and poured in some more…this time none came out the other end. The moist earth was now able to catch and hold all that I poured in. That's when I saw a beautiful illustration of my spiritual life.

There are times when I'm in a dry season with God. Not praying but going through the motions without the emotions. I go to church and nothing sticks or moves me. I am just there. Nothing is penetrating or making a dent in my spirit. Everything goes straight over my head and I leave dissatisfied, grouchy even.

I was relying on the worship to stir something inside of me and it didn't. The message bounced off my spirit and sounded like a foreign language. I brought nothing in, and I took nothing away. I was unable to absorb anything because my spirit was too dry to receive it.

Finally, in desperation to lay hold of God again, I get away for a quiet time with Him. Away from all that distracts me, I make myself stay in the presence of God until I feel His touch again. I weep, I cry, I wail. I pour out my emotions and thoughts. All the pain, angst, and disappointment rush over the dam. And God comes. He's been waiting…waiting for me to get to the well, to the place where I choose to seek Him. He washes me, restores me, refills me, and refreshes me. He also renews my hopes, corrects my faulty views, and gives me wisdom for moving forward. I carry that precious time in my heart, allowing it to spring up in my spirit when I'm tempted to go down the road that eventually leads back to the same desert place. I *choose to worship* in spite of how I feel. I *choose to saturate my spirit with praise for God* and walk out His Word, even when I don't see any immediate blessings.

The next time I go to church, everything is fresh again. The worship washes over me, joining what I've already stirred up in my spirit. The study of God's Word confirms everything that He has whispered to me. I feel new, hopeful, alive. Yes, God still loves me! He's still here beside me. I am not forgotten.

This is the cycle of spiritual living for most of us. Seasons of great intimacy with God are often followed by times when we feel disconnected from Him. He hasn't moved; we have. He's always with us, inviting us to grow a little more, to stretch our spiritual wings a little wider, to go a step further than we're used to. Growing, stretching, stepping out until we are able to fly.

Again and again throughout Scripture we see repeat visits from Christ. Another touch applied. Another reminder of His love. God urges us to become consistent with Him. To make Him a priority as we would any relationship that is significant. We can quibble about what time of day we need to pray and have quiet times if we want, but the important thing is to make them happen every day. God needs to be our first priority. As we give Him the first fruits of our labor, why not give him the first of our day?

Get your marching orders for the day and be prepared to meet the world. Jesus prayed to His heavenly Father daily. In His Father's presence He gained the strength and insights for each day and the various encounters He would experience.

When Jesus taught His disciples how to pray, consistency was included: "Give us this day our daily bread" (Matthew 6:11). There are many daily rituals we partake in that can remind us to remember our spiritual health.

- Daily you wash. Allow God to wash and saturate you with His Word daily.

- Daily you get dressed. Put on the armor of God every day (Ephesians 6). You need every part to make it in this world.

The helmet of salvation to keep you in a godly mindset. The breastplate of righteousness to keep your heart in right-standing with God. Take up your sword because the Word of God will equip you for every battle and help you slay dragons. Your shield of faith helps extinguish every arrow that threatens to deflate your hope and kill your spirit. Gird yourself with truth, the belt that keeps everything in place. Yes, get dressed every day inwardly and outwardly.

- Daily you feed your body. Make sure you read God's Word daily to nourish your spirit.
- Daily you choose to do the right things. Daily you need to die to those things that threaten to rule your flesh. The apostle Paul said, "I die daily" (1 Corinthians 15:33).

Some nutritionists encourage us to drink as much water in ounces as we have body weight because our bodies are mostly water. Perhaps the same rule should apply spiritually, that we need to drink deeply from God continuously until He saturates our souls with Himself. In Him we breathe, move, and have our very being. So pray and make melodies in your heart continually, keeping Jesus' living water flowing constantly.

Go to the well, my sister! Go as many times as you can and have to. At the end of the day, in Christ alone we live and hope.

Reflections

1. What does your relationship with God look like?

2. In what areas could it improve?

3. *What disciplines can you put in place to be more consistent in connecting with God?*

4. *What distractions will make this difficult for you? What can you do to eliminate them?*

5. *What can you "fast from" or choose not to do for 30 days to make time and room for a consistent meeting with God? (I'm trying to help you form a habit of prayer.)*

Refreshing Springs

The world has made the idea of being dependent a negative. Yet God created you for relationship and built into the core of your spirit a need for Him. All human relationships have their moments of disappointment, such as when a loved one lets you down. But your relationship with God doesn't have that aspect. He wants to fellowship with you consistently, and He will always respond to you. He will never leave you nor forsake you. He is with you forever. Praise His holy name!

Refreshing Reminders

- When the heat is on in our lives, it always reveals who we really are.

- We will always be asked to give what we are in search of ourselves. It is in the giving that we receive. In ministering we are ministered to.

- God will always ask questions that will cause us to see our lack and our need for Him.

- Weariness and disappointment can magnify our lack and cause us to concentrate on that instead of what is truly important—our relationship with God.

- When people are magnified in our eyes, we tend to belittle ourselves or become overly critical of others. Comparison is a deadly game that no one wins.

- We are the only ones who can disqualify ourselves from being blessed by God.

- Faith always involves risk, but in Christ we have a guaranteed positive end.

- Our perception of God's intentions toward us will determine the choices we make.

- To be set free, we have to be honest about where we really are now.

- Jesus will always make us locate ourselves. He will not address what we won't confess. In other words, He waits for us to ask for His help. He won't fix what we won't admit.

- The vows we make to protect ourselves can become prisons that keep us away from the very things we long for.

- We have to be willing to release the old to receive what God has in store for us.

- Once you have a revelation of who Jesus is and who He is to you, you will let go of what you thought you wanted and grasp what you really need—Him!

- Worship is a lifestyle. It is not isolated to a single act.

- To receive the blessings God has for us, we need to be willing to let go of our expectations and remain open to His greater good for our lives.

- God is a God of process. With every trial we experience He grants us the opportunity to transform our pain into power.

- Passion and influence are two power tools that women hold, but we must learn to use them wisely.

- We have a God-sized hole in our hearts. God is waiting for our invitation to fill it with Him.

- Our struggle with holiness is because of our brokenness. As we mature spiritually, we are able more and more to reflect God's holiness.

- Our lives are the greatest witness tool we have. They reveal the presence and redemptive work of Christ.

31 Thirst-quenching
Meditations

Day 1

*"There is hope for your future," declares the L*ORD.

JEREMIAH 31:17

I love the song "If Not for Grace." The writer asks the profound question of where I'd be if not for God's grace. I'd be a hopeless case and empty place. Thankfully, in spite of who we are and what we've done, God's grace brings hope to our lives.

Despite what we see before our eyes, have experienced in the past, or presently believe, there is hope. As long as God is on the throne of our lives, there is hope for us.

When repeat disappointments set into our lives, they can give the illusion that where we are presently is all we have to look forward to. That can be a very bleak picture of nothingness stretching endlessly to the horizon of our lives. This is a desert place. But God will always place a well of refreshing water somewhere. A place where our spirits can go to drink deep and freshen our hearts. If we've lived our lives with any degree of passion, if we've taken risks, if we've followed our dreams, if we've lived long enough to experience heartaches, there will come times when we will hit a wall, throw up our hands, and know we can't go any further in our own strength. That is when Jesus meets you where you are, extending His hand of friendship and love. Take it, my dear sister, and let Him help you. Dare to hope again.

Heavenly Father, I am so tired. I have come to the end of myself and can go no further. There are no words left to pray except I need You to meet me in this place. Come to my rescue. Grant me Your wisdom and Your strength. Help my unbelief and renew my hope in You. In Jesus' name I pray. Amen.

Day 2

Hope deferred makes the heart sick,
but desire fulfilled is a tree of life.
PROVERBS 13:12

Hold on a little while longer. Even in this hard time God knows how you feel. Your heart can grow weak from the constant assaults. Life takes its toll emotionally, spiritually, and physically. Depression isn't just emotional, it can be physiological as well. Whether you are in the camp of the woman at the well who had weathered the disappointments of life and love or you are like Elijah, exhausted from the battle of working for the kingdom of God, you need to make your way to the well of God's vast supply of living water to achieve true restoration.

The truth is that in the process of life we usually experience the worst before we get to partake of the best. Perhaps in God's wisdom He knows that broken vessels treasure what is poured into them more. He knows we have experienced what it is like to be without, so we know what life and joy can cost.

God also has perfect timing. He will not let us die on the vine. He will water us and tend to us in such a way that our trials will produce fruit. And not just for our benefit! He will make us a vessel of blessings to others. Oh how quickly we can forget the struggles when the blessings come, especially if we are not tempered by our experiences and the lessons learned along the way. God knows this. He will not let us die in despair. So hold on and look forward to new life in Him!

Heavenly Father, I am waiting on You. Restore my life and water my soul. Though my hopes have not been realized, I know You know my needs and will provide for them at the right time. Come quickly, Lord! In Jesus' name. Amen.

Day 3

When doubts filled my mind, your comfort
gave me renewed hope and cheer.
PSALM 94:19 NLT

If you have doubts, you are not alone. The psalmist experienced that too. Jesus promised us a Comforter. He also promised to give His peace and joy to us. These can't be taken away, no matter what happens in this life.

Certain truths remain unshakeable for those who believe in Jesus Christ. Though life screams loudly, the voice of God often comes softly. Perhaps on purpose so we will quiet our spirits and listen. The voices that accuse us of messing up or point out our stupid mistakes and embarrassing failures want to distract us from the still, small voice of God.

Nothing is too big for God to handle. Nothing is so off putting to Him that He won't draw close and embrace us, soothe us, and remind us of His promises. And He always keeps them! He is faithful, consistent, and divinely patient. We can't "blow it" with Him. In fact, blowing it might be a good thing if it brings us to our knees in front of our Lord and Savior. That is where healing begins. He gathers us to Him and gives us glimpses of our future in Him. He surprises us with joy and peace in the most surprising places. Though nothing has changed externally, we are renewed within. And that brings the peace that surpasses all understanding.

Heavenly Father, draw me close to You and be my comfort. Heal my heart and make me whole in You. I need Your peace and Your joy to fill me and sustain me. As I rest in Your arms, be more real to me than ever before. In Jesus' name. Amen.

Day 4

This I recall to my mind, therefore I have hope.
LAMENTATIONS 3:21

Do you remember what God did before in your life? He will do it again. Life is seasonal—summer, fall, winter, spring—and each season has a marked impact on our lives. Sometimes in the midst of winter, we survey the death of all things dear—relationships, dreams, whatever is near and dear to our hearts—and wonder what good can come from something so disappointing But then spring comes, bringing newness of life and we laugh and love again, we dare to take another risk, we live out our dreams. We say, "Isn't that something? God knew all along." That is the trophy we must keep in our case.

Remember a time when God came through for you? When it looked like there was no way you were going to make it? When there was no way life could be breathed back into your heart? But that changed, just like the seasons change. Nothing remains the same except God. This trial too shall pass, and God will reveal His work in it. That's another facet of His goodness and faithfulness. He is passionate in His love for you. He will not let you stay ashamed. He will not leave you in despair. He will not forsake you. In those moments when you wonder where God is, think back...back to when He showed up for you the last time you were in a tight or difficult spot. Trust Him to do it again.

Heavenly Father, please forgive me for not trusting You more. Every time I come to a difficult place I doubt You. And yet You've proven You will come through for me every time. Help me exercise memories of You over present emotions so I will keep Your faithfulness in view. Help me rest in the knowledge of Your character. In Jesus' name. Amen.

Day 5

In [Jesus'] name shall the Gentiles hope.
ROMANS 15:12

What is in a name? Power—if it is the right name. Have you noticed how scandalized and uptight people become when the name of Jesus is mentioned? We can talk about Buddha, Muhammad, and other religious leaders all day long and no one will mind, but say the name of Jesus and the air goes out of the room. There is power in His name that can't be ignored. "At the name of Jesus every knee will bow...every tongue will confess that Jesus Christ is Lord" (Philippians 2:10). Every person and circumstance must bow to the name of Jesus!

What does this mean for you in the midst of your present circumstance? It means that whatever you are struggling with must bow to the name of Jesus—the name above all names and principalities, powers and dominions (Romans 8:38). The plans that the enemy of your soul has against you must give way at the name of Jesus. The war Satan has waged against your life, your heart, your spirit, your emotions must cease *when you invite Jesus into the midst of your pain, your disappointment, your questions.*

Before Jesus came to earth as a man, God pronounced that His name was "I Am"—and so He is. He is everything you need. He is healing, comfort, restoration, supply, mighty counselor, provider, lover of your soul. He is what you need, and He gives you hope. He will not leave you lonely, forsaken, or in distress. He will not leave you broken. No, He will mend your broken heart. He will collect your tears and soothe your pain. He will renew your heart to love again, to hope again, to believe again. His name alone gives you reason to hope.

Dear heavenly Father, my hope is in You through Your Son, Jesus. Thank You for being with me all the time and for working in my life. In Jesus' name. Amen.

Day 6

O Israel, hope in the Lord from
this time forth and forever.
Psalm 131:3

I f you've never hoped in God before, dare to hope now. Sometimes we say we believe, and then we waver when something happens in our lives that is negative and unexpected. We are rocked by the occurrence, and our faith gets rattled along with our psyches. This is when we see what we are truly made of and where we've placed our faith.

Perhaps you've put your hope where it doesn't belong? In a man, someone else's promise, yourself, your boss, your family, your achievements, or your finances. All these things will fail you. And the call from God is loud and clear: Redirect your misdirected faith. Set your sights on the One person who is able to do something about your situation and attitudes—God.

To magnify anything above Him is to set yourself up for further bruising. This is when your soul can become infected and your heart can become bitter. For most of us, expectations that have been dashed again and again because of the humanity of others make us question God. Remember that God is God, and He allows man to be man. Where you place your faith is your responsibility.

I encourage you to reassert your heart and fix your face toward the only perfect and consistent One who will never fail you. And if you haven't trusted God before, why not ask Jesus into your heart as your Lord and Savior now?

Dear heavenly Father, sometimes I choose specific areas of my life to hope for in You and leave the others up to me. Today I surrender everything—the totality of who I am and all that I hope for—into Your capable hands. Forgive me for compartmentalizing my faith. I'm choosing to trust You completely. In Jesus' name. Amen.

Day 7

The LORD takes pleasure in those who fear him,
in those who hope in his steadfast love.
PSALM 147:11 ESV

Awe and hope must coincide to secure faith. Awe comes from realizing the greatness of the One we revere—understanding His power, His abilities, and His good intentions toward us. When we celebrate the greatness of God and choose to trust in His love for us, He rises to the occasion to prove what we believe. To confirm, if you will, that our thoughts and beliefs are right and true. God cannot and will not disappoint us. He manifests His power to us—and not just to us but also to those who are watching our lives. He is more passionate about blessing us than we are to receive the blessings because they are opportunities for Him to glorify Himself and take our relationship with Him to another level.

Trials forge intimacy. When people go through things together, they get closer. They now have war stories to share about how they made it through difficult times by leaning on one another. The same is true with God. When He carries us through the hard times, it creates a personal history of His steadfast love and care for us that no one can take away. Imagine how His heart is warmed to know that we not only revere and honor Him, but we also trust Him implicitly based on what we've come through together. This is true intimacy that transcends "religion" because it comes from the heart.

Dear heavenly Father, I revere You. I stand in awe of Your glorious power. But most of all, I bow my heart in adoration, trusting in Your care for me. As I wait before You, please draw closer than close and let me feel Your presence and pleasure. In Jesus' name. Amen.

Day 8

I stretch out my hands to you; my soul thirsts
for you like a parched land.
PSALM 143:6 ESV

Picture in your mind Olympians running a race to win. Stretching, straining toward the finish line, anticipating the breaking of the ribbon, lean into the finish line tape. Why not lean into God like that? Anticipate His refreshing. The race of life will take a lot out of you, but God is faithful to restore you. To pour Himself out to fill you and to wash and renew you. When your spirit feels parched, you're dry from the inside out. Everything within you screams to be quenched. Reach out your hands to God.

The psalmist knew where to go when his spirit was thirsty. He compared his soul to the unending dry desert. Perhaps he had seen a mirage in his trek and run to it, anticipating delicious water only to find the relief he'd anticipated wasn't real. There are times in your life when you glimpse something that looks like what you need or want, but when you get up close you find it isn't real. You are disappointed, and your hopes are dashed. You wonder what will become of you. You see nothing good ahead.

In cases like that, don't look forward. Instead, look up! Stretch your arms upward and anticipate rain from heaven—cool and healing, filling and restoring. Filling in the cracks and saturating that which had hardened in the heat of life. God will pour the water and add His oil, rubbing it into your heart and weary spirit until you yield in His hands and invite His healing touch. Yes, lean in, break the ribbon, and fall into His arms.

Heavenly Father, I am weary and parched. I open my arms and reach
for You. Receive me and pour Your Spirit out that my thirst might be
quenched and my spirit renewed. In Jesus' name. Amen.

Day 9

God puts the fallen on their feet again and
pushes the wicked into the ditch.
PSALM 147:3 MSG

Jesus is the Master Physician. He knows where you hurt and exactly what you need to be healed. There is no guessing, no need for an x-ray, MRI, or other test. He sees all; He knows all. What is not obvious on the surface is revealed through the Holy Spirit, who searches the deep, dark corners of your heart and makes intercession for you in the will of the Father when you don't know how to pray. He exposes hidden scars and wounds and lays them bare before the Father, who lovingly gathers you up and binds you to Himself. Jesus, the skilled surgeon, then does His work by removing that which stands in the way of your healing. Tenderly He applies His healing balm and binds your wounds to protect them from further onslaught. This is what He is willing and able to do. This is what He does when you go to Him and simply ask.

Ask and you will receive, the Bible says. As you bring your brokenness to Him, He remains faithful to respond and heal. God is a gentleman, so He will not intrude on your pain if you don't invite Him to. But when you do, He is quick to answer. He said if you open the door, He will come in and sup with you. So press past your disappointment and even your unbelief. Show Him where it hurts. As the timeless hymn "What a Friend We Have in Jesus" says, "O what needless pain we bear, all because we do not carry, everything to God in prayer."

Dear heavenly Father, I bring my broken heart to You. Please apply Your healing touch. Look upon me; touch and restore me. My heart cries out to You. I place my hope in You for restoration. In Jesus' name. Amen.

Day 10

*The Lord will guide you continually and
satisfy your desire in scorched places and
make your bones strong.*

Isaiah 58:11 ESV

Do you feel yourself wilting in the midst of your situation? Do you no longer have the strength to stand, and if you do, you haven't the slightest idea which direction to move forward in? The issues of life can take a toll on your psyche, leaving you confused, desperate, directionless, tired, despondent, and lacking clarity. God knows and understands this. He instructs you that if you lack wisdom you are to ask Him, and He will freely counsel you without holding back or making you feel like an idiot. He will guide you through your desert place. He will grant clarity. He will strengthen you for the journey. He will give you the grace you need to do what you have to do. He will fill you with what you need and not allow you to lack anything if you look to Him as your source.

He is able to satisfy your desires in ways you can't anticipate. His ways are not your ways, and yet He makes a way out for you so you can experience rest from your trials and pain. He heals you—a deep inner healing that gets to the root of all you struggle with. He alone can satisfy you to the core, and He is faithful to answer every need and cry of your heart.

Dear heavenly Father, there are parts of me that only You can reach and fill. Touch me now. Renew my strength and lead me out of this place. Help me to once again experience the joy of my salvation in You. In Jesus' name. Amen.

Day 11

*You shall be like a watered garden, like a spring
of water, whose waters do not fail.*

ISAIAH 58:11 ESV

God wants to saturate your life with Himself. To fill every empty space with His Spirit and continually pour His refreshing on you. He calls you to walk under an open heaven that rains blessings and favors on your life.

In times when it feels heaven has closed and the rain has ceased, He calls you to dig deeper. To look within and find Him abiding in you, releasing fresh springs to cleanse, wash, heal, and restore. He hydrates your spirit and quenches your thirsty soul. Stir up the gift that is within you. Follow the stream within, vast and unending because its origin is not of this earth. It comes straight from the throne of the Father who has an endless supply of what you need.

He will not allow you to suffer lack if you believe in Him and serve Him. When the heat is on, He releases more of His sustaining strength to help you make it to the other side of the trial, the other side of your pain. This is supernatural. People may wonder how you are doing so well in the midst of your circumstances. You may even seem to be thriving! God has said you will flourish in the midst of famine (Romans 8:35-37). This is not just physical well-being. There are seasons when you will experience a famine of the soul, when your heart is bereft. This is the place God visits, pouring out His love and filling the parched areas with His healing waters. He keeps pouring until you are overflowing and wanting no more. Like a garden well tended, this is where lush fruit grows that blesses you and others.

*Heavenly Father, I am thirsty. Please saturate me with You and feed
me Your life-giving grace and strength. In Jesus' name. Amen.*

Day 12

*With joy you will draw water
from the wells of salvation.*

Isaiah 12:3

God wants you to know that you have an endless supply of love and help to draw from when you need it. What He does not pour out for you, you can draw for yourself by asking Him. Everyone needs a different measure of His refreshing. Take what you need. His joy will be your strength, empowering you to reach for more of Him and all that He is until you are overflowing with His goodness, provision, healing, and deliverance. He will fill your heart with hope and your mouth with laughter. He promises to give you joy—not the type the world gives that is temporary at best and subject to external stimuli. No, we're talking about the kind of joy that doesn't rely on anything other than the Spirit of God to preserve it. When your joy originates in Him, it won't be deflated by temporal circumstances. The joy He gives is unwavering because it rests on His constancy. Because He abides in you, so does His joy.

As you drink from His well of salvation, you increase in strength. Yes, as Nehemiah 8:10 says, "The joy of the Lord is your strength!" You will sense God's favor as you return to Him. He smiles as you experience anew His grace and mercy. Drink in His comfort and glory knowing He is here for you. You can return and draw from Him time and time again! His love and compassion will never fail you, so drink in, drink deep, and then drink again.

Dear heavenly Father, I thirst for Your joy. Ease my pain and fill my mouth with laughter. Return to me the joy of my salvation, and I will praise You and tell others of Your goodness and healing. In Jesus' name. Amen.

*[The LORD says,] "I'll show up and take care of you
as I promised and bring you back home.
I know what I'm doing. I have it all planned out—
plans to take care of you, not abandon you,
plans to give you the future you hope for."*

JEREMIAH 29:10-11 MSG

*"I know the plans I have for you," says the LORD.
"They are plans for good and not for disaster,
to give you a future and a hope."*

JEREMIAH 29:11 NLT

*"I know what I have planned for you," says the LORD.
"I have plans to prosper you, not to harm you.
I have plans to give you a future filled with hope."*

JEREMIAH 29:11 ESV

Another translation for Jeremiah 29:10-11 says that God has a predetermined end in mind for us. That end is victory! Just how we will get there isn't always clear to our human minds and hearts. Although God knows the plans He has for us, we don't always know what He is up to. He does assure us that He knows what He is doing. In Him alone should we rest and trust. He loves us. He wants what is best for us. He is a God of process that uses every part of our lives to create a glorious picture. Like a good movie with plot twists and turns, villains and heroes, our lives stretch out before us in epic proportions. We win, we lose, we hurt, we dare to believe again. And at the helm of our personal movie is God—the writer, producer, and director. He knows the end of our stories. He knows the purpose is to help us become like Jesus and glorify Him.

When the drama begins in your life, remember this is the beginning of an amazing story!

Dear heavenly Father, help me trust You more, even in those moments when I can't see Your hand at work. Help me rest in Your love and care, knowing You are all-powerful. In Jesus' name. Amen.

Day 14

We rejoice in our sufferings, knowing that
suffering produces endurance, and endurance produces character,
and character produces hope, and
hope does not put us to shame, because
God's love has been poured into our hearts through
the Holy Spirit who has been given to us.
ROMANS 5:3-5 ESV

God loves us so much that He allows us to suffer. Strange but true. He has His eye on the big picture of our lives. His passion is to create character in us. The type of character that will weather the storms of life just like the sturdy trees of Lebanon. These trees have stood the test of time being bowed over, bent by strong winds, and then straightened and strengthened by the sap that is released from those stress points. This makes them one of the most durable woods in the world. We are like that! Though we are broken we don't remain so. The balm of the Holy Spirit is released, producing spiritual muscles we wouldn't get any other way. In the midst of our brokenness, God shows His strength, giving us a track record we can trust.

Because life is cyclical we come to know He is faithful. With His support, we learn to stand through the various setbacks we experience. We know He is with us. We know He will restore us. We know that anything worth keeping is never lost in Christ. Based on what we learn (often learned the hard way), we trust Him more consistently. We tend to panic less because we've been to this place before and we know the outcome. We endure and trust based on the sufficiency of our faithful God. What a beautiful place to live.

Dear heavenly Father, grant me the strength to endure. Let my charac-
ter reflect Your faithfulness as I learn to trust You more. In Jesus' name.
Amen.

Day 15

Come, all you who are thirsty, come to the waters; and
you who have no money, come, buy and eat!
Come, buy wine and milk without money and without cost.
ISAIAH 55:1 NIV

Life can be expensive. And yet God, who holds that which is priceless in His hands, offers free sustenance to everyone who wants it. Consider the cost of the things you long for in life. Love will cost you everything. Your dreams might cost you everything to pursue them. And then there is salvation, when God offers a respite to the soul too weary to fend for itself. To the person who is out of resources, whose heart has bled and been left empty, He says, "Come! I won't charge you. I've already paid the debt for you. Come and drink freely. Eat and be filled. Rest a while and gain your strength for the journey."

And God doesn't end there; this is just the beginning. Every new trial introduces you to a new level of life and love. You equip yourself for moving forward by building up your inner self with the sustenance only God can give—His salvation. His redemption is an expensive meal, and yet He says come and eat for free! Drink the milk and strengthen your bones, drink the wine and let your stomach be settled and your spirit cheered. Beyond this, know once and for all that God will not leave you wanting.

Dear heavenly Father, I come to You with empty hands to receive all You have to offer. Fill me with You. When I feel I need more, grant me more of You. In Jesus' name. Amen.

Day 16

He satisfies the longing soul, and the
hungry soul he fills with good things.
PSALM 107:9 ESV

What are you longing for? So many times I've pursued things that didn't satisfy as I imagined they would. Fleeting moments of temporary gratification left me more empty than before. Tasting but not tasting satisfaction leaves an even greater chasm in our souls because we're at a loss about what will ultimately satisfy us. And yet God knows exactly what will hit the spot. And He wants to give it to us! Time and time again He surprises us with His joy. He fills us to overflowing with good things that aren't always obvious to our human eyes.

Canceling out our bad choices, our mistakes, and our flaws, God replaces them with Himself. He shifts our focus from the temporal to the everlasting, softening and then dismissing our momentary disappointments with a greater promise. At His throne are pleasures—eternal pleasures. But we also have the earthly pleasure now of knowing God is here for us and ready to satisfy the longings of our hearts. He is present in our day-to-day, giving us our daily bread. And often we find that although nothing has changed around us, we have changed within. We are whole and satisfied in our loving heavenly Father.

Dear heavenly Father, thank You for the bread of life You extended to me. Thank You for answering the longings of my soul. You alone know what I truly need. As I delight myself in You, I wait in expectancy for You to grant the desires of my heart. In Jesus' name. Amen.

Day 17

A person who is full refuses honey, but even bitter food tastes sweet to the hungry.

PROVERBS 27:7 NLT

Even a hungry dog will sniff a bone before he eats it. It's called self-preservation. We make sure food is safe to eat before putting it into our bodies. Yet depending on what we think we lack or how long we've been waiting for our desire to be filled, sometimes the first glimpse of anything that resembles what we've been hoping for can cause us to rush to embrace it. It's called desperation.

When left to my own devices I, like Eve, often choose what isn't God's best for me. I allow the serpent to convince me that I hunger for something that won't really nourish me. But when I allow God to fill me with Himself, I am far more discerning. Satisfaction is wonderful. It stabilizes my heart and gives me clarity. This is why God can't be tempted. He is His own sufficiency. Whole and holy. Everything He desires is within Him.

As we live, move, and breathe in Him, we are filled with His sufficiency and protected against temptation. There is nothing left to desire outside of Him and His will for our lives. When we are walking with Him, our desires change and we are set free from wanting the things that steal our joy, peace, and wholeness. This is kingdom living!

Dear heavenly Father, save me from desperation. Fill me until I want no more. Let me find my sufficiency in You and You alone. In Jesus' name. Amen.

Day 18

Jesus declared, "I am the bread of life. He who comes to me will never go hungry, and he who believes in me will never be thirsty."

JOHN 6:35 NIV

The key to being filled is to take your emptiness to Him. Jesus is a gentleman, He will not force Himself on you. He will not force you to eat what He longs to provide. He knows your hunger, but He waits patiently for you to come to Him. He knows your thirst, and He stands ready to quench the fire in your throat when you call. He stands at the door and knocks, waiting for you to answer and invite Him in.

And what a wonderful guest He is! He comes bearing food and the liquid libation that will complement the meal. His Word is milk, bread, and meat. Milk and bread if you are just starting out with Him and meat when you're ready for more. God brings health and strength as you partake of His Word. He rewards those who seek Him diligently and consistently.

Daily bread is dispensed from His hand, and cooling water continually flows. It is delicious fare given freely when you come to Him. He is so generous! There is no greater satisfaction than feasting on what He provides. He is sustenance that nourishes and strengthens. You will not experience hunger pangs in a few hours as you do with natural food. God's ability to fill you and quench your thirst is supernatural, divine, settling your heart and answering your needs once and for all.

As you seek Him daily, He refills you again and again, filling every empty space in your heart and soul.

Dear heavenly Father, I reach out to You, bringing my emptiness and my thirst. Feed me with You until I hunger no more. In Jesus' name. Amen.

Day 19

*I have given rest to the weary and
joy to the sorrowing.*
JEREMIAH 31:25

God will not leave you broken. He will not leave you dry and weary. He doesn't overlook you when you're tired of the challenges of life. He draws near, bringing His rivers of peace and restoration when you call on Him. He hears the cry of your heart and the longing of your spirit. He comes to dry your tears and bring you His special brand of comfort.

He brings good and perfect gifts—food for the soul and every provision needed to fill you and renew you. He sees the empty places inside you, the places that have been torn in your heart. The rips in your soul. He applies His healing balm and releases His healing energy and sustenance. Understanding is released, filling the blanks in your life and equipping you to move forward.

Besides comfort, God gives you directions for moving forward while giving strength to your body and bones. There will be no withering on the vine when He tends to your heart. He gives you all you need to grow strong and bear good fruit.

Dear heavenly Father, I choose to abide in You and draw all I need from You. In You I live and breathe and have my being. In You I am completely satisfied. I rest in this knowledge and look to You for sustenance. In Jesus' name. Amen.

Day 20

You keep track of all my sorrows.
You have collected all my tears in your bottle.
You have recorded each one in your book.
PSALM 56:8 NLT

How amazing that the God of the universe, the alpha and omega, the Lord of all Creation looks down on us and draws close enough to collect our tears and keep them in a bottle. What a tender picture of compassion the psalmist paints by giving us a glimpse into God's heart. Our God is so tender that He watches over us as we toss and turn at night. He feels our angst; He empathizes with our inner turmoil. He holds us while we despair, offering His comfort. We are so precious to Him that He will not allow even one tear to fall to the ground. He catches every one and keeps them, absorbing our pain and making it His own. He has taken note of our sorrows, numbering our tears and tracking the length of our suffering.

Do you find this comforting? I know there are times when you may feel forgotten or even wonder if God cares. Perhaps you debate whether He can relate to what you're going through. Or maybe you even think He is the source of your suffering. In His Word, God clearly states He *does not* enjoy your pain. He says He will be right there with you, holding you, comforting you, whispering secrets of restoration to you.

No, my sister, you have not been overlooked or tossed aside. Your pain is as real to God as it is to you. He cares, He grieves with you, and He waits to fill your mouth with laughter and your heart with joy once again. In times like these you need to go to the Bible and meditate on the promises and reminders that God loves you with an everlasting love and waits to carry you through your experience to the place where restoration awaits.

Dear heavenly Father, I am comforted by knowing You care. Thank You! In Jesus' name. Amen.

Day 21

The Spirit and the bride say, "Come!"
And let him who hears say, "Come!"
Whoever is thirsty, let him come; and whoever wishes,
let him take the free gift of the water of life.
REVELATION 22:17 NIV

Do you wonder if you qualify for the gifts God gives? Wonder no more! You do! God clearly states that whoever wishes to receive His gifts only needs to come to Him. He does not categorize us according to who we are, what we've done, or how shallow or deep our sins may be. He is an equal opportunity God!

If you are thirsty, come. If you are hungry, come. If you have sinned, come. If you have made a mess of your life, come. And there is no price attached to the gifts of life He gives. The only cost is your surrender. When you come to Him, you will inevitably leave some things behind...and you'll lose some things along your journey. What are these? The objects, behaviors, and attitudes that kept you bound. That hindered your faith and destroyed your hope. When you come to Him, you will let go of some things—and perhaps even some people who keep you from experiencing all God has for you. You will also gain! God won't leave you empty-handed. For every thing you let go of, He will replace it with Himself. He will replace all you release with much better fare at no additional cost to you. He has already absorbed the price through the blood of His Son Jesus. Your salvation was a free gift but an expensive one for Him. Don't take His precious sacrifice for granted. Joyfully embrace it and treasure it. Thank Him for all He's done to give you life, love, and freedom in Him.

Dear heavenly Father, I humbly accept Your great and precious gifts of salvation, peace, joy, and even the hardships that will help me grow strong in You. In Jesus' name. Amen.

Day 22

"Come now, let us reason together," says the LORD.
*"Though your sins are like scarlet, they shall be
as white as snow; though they are red as crimson,
they shall be like wool."*

ISAIAH 1:18 NIV

There is no failure, mistake, or stain too deep to be redeemed by the hand of our loving and merciful God. In the midst of our disappointments and failures He invites us to come and discuss the matter with Him. He is a reasonable God. In the atmosphere of truth He will help us get to the bottom of the problem and find a solution. He isn't put off by sin as much as He is put off by a lack of willingness on our part to own our sins and errors. If we will be honest, He will show us the way. But if we are proud, He will resist reaching out.

God gives grace to the humble, to those willing to come before Him and stretch out their dirty hands asking for cleansing. A contrite and remorseful spirit brings out the tenderness in Him. He doesn't want to rub salt in our wounds or even accuse us. He wants to gently wash us, to wipe away the pain and disappointments. He wants to renew our hope. By His spirit He will remove the stains from our souls and make us new.

*Dear heavenly Father, I come to You ready to face the truth of who I
am and the truths of Your Word. Please wash me and make me new
in You. In Jesus' name. Amen.*

Day 23

Blessed are those who hunger and thirst
for righteousness, for they shall be satisfied.
MATTHEW 5:6

We hunger and thirst for a lot of things and try to satisfy our desires... but come up feeling emptier than ever. Are we hungering and thirsting for the wrong things? The problem with being human is that we tend to be short-sighted about eternity, placing it low on our lists of priorities. Heavenly matters don't seem as urgent when so many people and projects are pressing for our attention here. And yet the cries of our hearts and the hunger of our souls shouldn't be ignored. They will grow more insistent as the days go by. Eventually we have to stop and pay attention to the spirit inside each of us, which is really the convicting presence of the Holy Spirit.

I've discovered that when I place God first, everything else falls into line and into the right perspective. Life stops being a successful bully when we pay attention to and serve a different master! I encourage you to deliberately choose to make Christ Lord in your life every day. Continually seek to improve your relationship with Him. Right-standing with Him is *the* guarantee of a happy ending.

Dear heavenly Father, there is no righteousness in me. Thank You for sharing Yours. Please fill me with You so that I may be totally whole. In Jesus' name. Amen.

Day 24

I urge you... in view of God's mercy,
to offer your bodies as living sacrifices,
holy and pleasing to God—this is your spiritual act of worship.
ROMANS 12:1

Does offering your body as a living sacrifice seem extreme to you? In light of all God has given, isn't it really perfect and reasonable to strive to live holy before Him? This isn't to seek His blessing. No, it's a way of saying thank you for the severe sacrifice God made by asking His Son Jesus to die for our sins so we could enter into a personal relationship with Him.

When I think of God's goodness I'm so humbled. In spite of me, in spite of all the foolish choices I've made, in spite of all the mistakes I've repeated, and in spite of all the times I've questioned His actions, God remains faithful to love me and provide for me.

When my life gets off balance I'm reminded of His love for me, and then I remember Jesus Christ is the same yesterday and today and forever (Hebrews 13:8). He hasn't changed or moved so I must have. Once again I revisit His Word, looking into His perfect law and examining life from His viewpoint. His ways are not our ways; His thoughts are not our thoughts (Isaiah 55:8). We must press into the heart of God to acquire His mindset. As our thoughts change to more closely resemble His, so will our words and actions. That is when we truly see God at work and experience more consistent victories, when we truly let our lives reflect and serve Him.

Even though we know it's not profitable to continue to insist on our own way, we continue to do it. Let's purpose today to turn to God, crawl back up on the altar, and offer our lives and bodies to Him. This is where we will find rest.

Dear heavenly Father, I struggle to give up my will and my desires. As I go through the day, help me focus on You and what You want to accomplish through me. I surrender all of me so I can be filled with You. In Jesus' name. Amen.

Jesus said to them, "My food is to do the will
of him who sent me and to accomplish his work."
JOHN 4:34

For so many years I struggled in one love relationship after another as I tried to fill the void within. I was seeking acceptance and validation. When that failed, I turned to my career, believing that garnering the admiration of others and professional accolades would do the trick. That failed too.

Then along the path of self-determination I came to the end of what I could accomplish. I was introduced to Jesus, and I surrendered to His will for my life. By following His instructions I was surprised to discover more joy than I ever imagined existed. Suddenly life was overwhelmingly fulfilling. Then I realized the awesome discovery that the hole in my heart wasn't about a person, an achievement, or even an acquisition. The hole in my heart was God-sized. I hungered to be filled with God, to be in the center of doing His will, which is what I was created to do. It was a purpose-sized hole that could be filled with nothing but God. No wonder nothing ever satisfied me for long. Can you relate?

As I began to touch the lives of people for God, I would forget to eat. Like Jesus, I was focused on a different kind of food. This heavenly food fed my spirit, my mind, and my heart. I felt alive and was given the great blessing of sharing the bread of life with others. The more I opened myself to be a vessel of God's love and wisdom, the more purposeful and significant I felt. No longer did I need the validation of others. I was about the business of pleasing my heavenly Father.

Heavenly Father, my will is to do Your will. I want to complete the assignments You give me in a way that will please You, bless me, and introduce people to You. In Jesus' name. Amen.

Day 26

Why do you spend money for what is not bread,
and your wages for what does not satisfy?
Listen carefully to Me, and eat what is good,
and delight yourself in abundance.

ISAIAH 55:2

We get caught up in the tyranny of the urgent so easily, don't we? We're distracted by all that feeds the flesh until we find we're out of balance and unfulfilled because that food isn't nourishing. We spend our energy chasing careers and achievements only to find they don't satisfy. When we find ourselves in a heap of disappointment and wondering if this is all there is, we need to quiet ourselves and get before God.

When we cry out to Him, He will show us what is truly important, what will satisfy our souls, what will heal us, and what will refresh us. Not only will He prepare a delicious and nutritious meal to feed us…He's going to make it a feast. He promises to serve us abundant food. The sustenance He serves will not only be good *to* us, but it will also be good *for* us. I like the sound of that!

With all the talk of things that are good for us, it's easy to turn up our noses and fool ourselves into believing what God is going to serve will be about as exciting as broccoli. Have you noticed something interesting about food that is good for us? It is an *acquired* taste. As we adjust our diets to His food, we'll be developing heavenly tastes and learning to feast on God's goodness. There are no empty calories, and the taste is out of this world!

Dear heavenly Father, thank You for inviting me to Your table. I want to feast on Your goodness and become more like You. In Jesus' name. Amen.

Day 27

*[Jesus] answered, "It is written, 'Man shall not
live by bread alone, but by every word
that comes from the mouth of God.' "*

MATTHEW 4:4 ESV

How many different ways do we seek to fill our empty souls? Perhaps that is why we frustrate ourselves so much. When I realize I've been looking everywhere but to God, I picture Him sitting, waiting patiently. I stand before Him, bloated in my own efforts to fill the chasm within. He simply asks, "Have you had enough? If you haven't feasted on my Word, you won't be satisfied. My Word is the missing ingredient in your life. Without it, life isn't sustainable. You will lack direction."

Yes, you need natural food, but you also need to feed your spirit even more than you feed your body. What you feed the most in your life will be the strongest, so hang on to God's every word. Not *some* of His Word; *all* of it. Take it all in. Let it feed you. Let it renew your mind. Let it rearrange your priorities, your sensibilities, how you live your life. You are what you eat. It is absorbed into your being and manifests itself in your skin, your posture, your energy, and your strength level. What you consume determines the quality of your life. Will you be strong or vulnerable to affliction? How strong will your immune system be? A good life comes from a life well lived. To live well you need the direction of the Word. God says, "Ask where the good way is, and walk in it" (Jeremiah 6:16). You can't live truly satisfied in your own strength. When you come to the end of yourself, that's where God begins—if you've chosen to consume the food He's provided.

*Dear heavenly Father, let Your Word fill me with life and wisdom so
that I can live as You created me to. In Jesus' name. Amen.*

Day 28

*Do not merely listen to the word, and so
deceive yourselves. Do what it says.
Anyone who listens to the word but does not do what it says is
like a man who looks at his face in a mirror and, after looking at himself,
goes away and immediately forgets what he looks like.
But the man who looks intently into the perfect law that
gives freedom, and continues to do this, not forgetting what he has heard,
but doing it—he will be blessed in what he does.*

JAMES 1:22-25 NIV

As Paul the apostle noted to Timothy, there are certain weak-willed people (he actually called them silly women), who will be forever learning but never coming to the knowledge of the truth. These people would rather learn and gather information without applying it. Their insistence on going their own way means they never adjust their lives in light of the Word of God. And then they blame God for the consequences of their choices and actions. The Bible clearly tells us to look at ourselves. We're to lean forward in the mirror of God's Word and take a good hard look with the willingness to be honest about what we see.

Have you done that? If not, why not do it right now? And if God points something out to you, welcome the correction or suggested change. Don't grow angry and resist. "The Lord disciplines those he loves" (Hebrews 12:11). He is treating you as His beloved daughter. Trust Him. Let Him show you how you really are, and then let Him show you the person He created you to be. Yield to what He reveals, and allow Him to give you a perfect makeover.

Dear heavenly Father, I can't wait to see the me I will become as I apply Your Word to my life more consistently. Touch me and make me a beautiful reflection of You. In Jesus' name. Amen.

Day 29

Jerusalem will be known as "The Desirable Place"
and "The City No Longer Forsaken."

ISAIAH 62:12 NLT

Your new name will be "The City of God's Delight's"
and "The Bride of God," for the LORD delights in you
and will claim you as his bride.

ISAIAH 62:4 NLT

You are not alone. You belong to the Lord of lords and the King of kings! He claims you as His own. No longer do you need to wonder about your worth. God has deemed you priceless and purchased you with the life of His Son. The past is a former reality; your new life is joy and completion in Him. He will wash away your tears, and He will crown you with restoration and salvation. He dances in His delight to claim you as His own. Ha! Just think, the most royal of kings is delighted that you are His. He has no shame in claiming you—He does it openly and with great joy.

All the negative things people have said to you are banished in the light of what He declares over your life. You are no longer a cast-off. You are spoken for. You are loved. You are the apple of His eye and highly desired. You are the bride of Christ. You are not loveless; you are surrounded by the Lover of your soul. You are a member of "a royal priesthood, a holy nation, a people belonging to God, that you may declare the praises of him who called you out of darkness into His wonderful light" (1 Peter 2:9 NIV). You are set apart and on a special assignment to glorify God, to manifest His presence and power on earth, to be an accurate reflection of Him.

There is no room for feelings of inferiority or failure. He has filled those places in your life with Himself and taken up your part. Old things have passed away; all things have become new (see 2 Corinthians 5:17). Cast off your despair, friend. Look up to Jesus and live!

Heavenly Father, thank You for giving me a new beginning. In Jesus' name. Amen.

Day 30

*Let your light shine before men in such a way that
they may see your good works, and
glorify your Father who is in heaven.*
MATTHEW 5:16

A loving daughter spends time with her father. She studies him. She knows what he loves and what he hates. She knows what makes him glad, mad, and sad. She knows his intentions and his inflections. A loving daughter also represents her father well. How are you doing as a loving daughter of the King of kings? Are you reflecting Him well?

God gives us the charge to go forth and let our lights shine. To be salt and light to a dying world. And make no mistake—the people of the world *are* watching. They have a lot to say about Christians. Though they may not have chosen God's path themselves, they believe they know how God's followers are supposed to behave and believe. When we falter in our Christian walk, God is misrepresented and His kingdom suffers reproach.

The ultimate measure of maturity as good daughters is how well we reflect our Father and His followers in public. Every day we get opportunities to be a credit to the kingdom. Now, I'm not issuing a call for perfection but for redirection on how we handle everyday life issues. The choices we make impact those around us. We are not exempt from suffering, but in Christ we have the power to react to difficulties differently. In our sufferings and setbacks we can shine brightly for Christ. I encourage you to decide not to be shaken by life. Instead, stand firm in your Father's promises and handle each challenge with grace. That is truly reflecting the Father.

*Dear heavenly Father, grant me the peace to stand firm in trials so
that Your beauty and grace will shine through me and draw others
to You. In Jesus' name. Amen.*

Day 31

*[Jesus said,] "Here on earth you will have many trials and sorrows.
But take heart, because I have overcome the world."*

JOHN 16:33 NLT

God is not shocked or rocked by any of the circumstances we encounter. He anticipated them all, and He stands ready to execute His plan for restoration at every turn. As we strive to get on top of our circumstances, our Father in heaven is already on top of them! Calmly and graciously He calls our chaos into order. Knowing this, we can count it all joy, realizing that every setback is a setup to help us get to a higher level of living in God, to a greater place of victory and expansion as we become accustomed to the seasons of life and walk in the confidence that God has our backs. There is no reason for worry, distress, or fear. Hasn't He proven Himself to us time and time again? He has already overcome everything that comes against us.

So be of good cheer. Don't ask why this situation happened to you. Instead, ask what God is revealing to you. What is He striving to get in or out of your life? In the face of this loss, what is He making room for? Instead of being discouraged, get excited about what God is teaching you. The greater the trial, the greater the joy that awaits.

Now is not the time to feel sorry for yourself and lapse into paralysis. Rise up, daughter of the King. Shake the dust off and break the yoke from your neck. Perhaps God has brought you to this place to teach you how to gird yourself up in the Holy Spirit and flex your prayer muscles. He knows the way you take, and He will meet you there. It doesn't matter if you can't always see Him. He is there and will show Himself in your hour of need. Walk in confidence and expectancy in Jesus.

Dear heavenly Father, I know I'm not exempt from suffering. Grant me the strength to weather the storms of life and come out with stronger faith and stamina in You. In Jesus' name. Amen.

Michelle McKinney Hammond

is a writer, singer, and speaker who focuses on improving love-driven relationships. She is the founder and president of HeartWing Ministries. She also cohosted the Emmy-nominated show *Aspiring Women* for many years. Michelle is the bestselling author of *101 Ways to Get and Keep His Attention; Secrets of an Irresistible Woman, What to Do Until Love Finds You;* and *The Power of Being a Woman.*

To correspond with Michelle McKinney Hammond, you may write to:

HeartWing Ministries
P.O. Box 11052
Chicago, IL 60611

E-mail her at heartwingmin@yahoo.com

or log on to her websites:
www.michellehammond.com
www.thedivaprinciple.com

For information on booking her for a speaking engagement, call:
1-866-391-0955
or log on to www.michellehammond.com

Other Books by
Michelle McKinney Hammond

101 Ways to Get and Keep His Attention
The DIVA Principle
How to Avoid the 10 Mistakes Single Women Make
How to Be Found by the Man You've Been Looking For
The Last Ten Percent (a novel)
Lessons from a Girl's Best Friend
The Power of Being a Woman
The Sassy Girl's Checklist for Living, Loving, and Overcoming
A Sassy Girl's Guide to Loving God
Sassy, Single, and Satisfied
Secrets of an Irresistible Woman
Single-Minded Devotion
What to Do Until Love Finds You
Why Do I Say "Yes" When I Need to Say "No"?

DVDs by Michelle
How to Get Past Disappointment DVD (180 min.)